HOLLY WELLS

All My Exes

First edition

Editing by Donna Marie West
Cover art by Stefan Prodanovic

This book was professionally typeset on Reedsy.
Find out more at reedsy.com

To my family, the village that helped me raise my daughter. I couldn't have done it without you and appreciate you more than you'll ever know.

To my daughter, Olivia. For being my reason to never give up.

To all my exes, if you never wanted me to say anything bad about you, then you should have been nicer to me.

To Karma, even though you take so long to come around, I thank you for delivering yourself to the people that deserve it.

Prologue

It's funny, you know. How you get to a state of well-being and happiness, and the universe finds a way of knocking you down just a bit to keep you in check. The situations and people I've left behind are rearing their ugly faces in my present life, forcing me to confront the pain of my past that I've tucked away in the deepest, darkest parts of my brain, never to be seen again. I've spent many hours untangling the foggy memories, filling in the blanks of what was completely forgotten, only to conclude that it was I who'd placed myself in every single one of those situations. I've shied away from taking accountability for the role I played in my part in my fucked-up past.

Until now.

As of late, things in my life have been coming full circle. I've spent the past twenty-some-odd years forgetting what I've gone through. Letting go of the anger of wasted time and effort, releasing the blame I placed on myself. I've attended countless therapy sessions, seeking reassurance that I wasn't to blame for the hardships I endured. Slowly but surely, I've come to accept the struggles of the life I've lived, both good and bad, as consequences of my own decisions. Multiple times I've found myself buried in depression and anxiety, trapped in a downhill spiral of self-doubt and worst-case scenarios. Yet through it all, I've learned that the only way to dig myself out of the mess I was in was to love and respect myself.

To make myself my highest priority.

A nearly impossible task.

Countless people have told me that I could write a book about all the experiences I've had. Even my therapist suggested that writing it all out might be the therapeutic outlet I needed. For someone who has always struggled with articulating my emotions, putting pen to paper seemed like a potentially liberating endeavor. Whether I wanted to share what I wrote or not was up to me. Following the advice of my therapist, I finally sat down with the ghosts of my past and embarked on this journey of self-discovery.

It wasn't until COVID-19 took over the world that I found the time and motivation to write my story. I found myself in another failed relationship, sitting in a hotel room that my sister paid for so I could hide and be safe. Alone with my thoughts, I asked myself the same old questions, searching for answers I already knew: *How many times do I have to go through something like this? Where did I go wrong?*

It was time to stop making excuses and start acknowledging the truth.

I like to think that everything I've gone through has made me a better person, made me who I am. I'm a firm believer that everything happens for a reason. But Jesus, was it all necessary? I could have gone without half of the bullshit and still turned out this way. I wonder why sometimes. Why me? But wondering gets you nowhere. Self-pity gets you nowhere. I would find myself bargaining with God, making side deals with Him in hopes for a smoother path. And when I saw the path only get bumpier, I would question life itself. But God doesn't give you anything you can't handle, right?

Yeah… Right.

I was born in a small town in northwest Indiana, just outside Chicago, in 1983. I grew up during two of the best decades to ever happen, in my opinion. The '80s and '90s produced some of the best music that is still being played on the radio today. The fashion trends from that era are making their way back to the Junior section at Target. Technology was on the brink of revolutionizing our future. Social media wasn't yet out there making people comfortable with disrespecting other people without the threat of being punched in the mouth. It really was a great time to be alive.

Our neighborhood and surrounding areas were filled with kids all around the same age as my sisters and me. We would all meet in front of our house to walk to school together, and we would spend our afternoons running around the neighborhood playing. A ravine bordered our cluster of houses, outlining the golf course that was on the other side. We would spend our weekends exploring the woods, catching frogs, and searching for golf balls to sell back to the golfers. This was probably one of my favorite things to do in the summer and one I didn't mind doing alone.

I often sought solitude to avoid the anxiety I felt when placed in social situations. However, if I ever needed to find anyone, all I had to do was walk around the block until I saw the pile of bicycles in front of someone's house. You didn't need to lock your doors at night. You could actually go to sleep with nothing but the storm door defending the entire house and all that was in it without any worry. It was a much simpler time in everyone's lives, and a time that I constantly wished to go back to.

I would go to bed dreaming of myself as an adult. Seeing

myself as a successful, attractive woman, only to wake up to the insecure "ugly duckling" who looked back at me in the mirror. I always felt out of place and never good enough, perpetually plagued by a sense of inadequacy, although I couldn't quite pinpoint why. Talking about feelings was a foreign concept in my family, so I found another way to express myself: I put it on paper in my drawings. I'd discovered I had a real talent for art, one that my parents were proud of. One that I would drown myself in when times got tough.

I relied on my three sisters to make friends in our younger years and then, as we got older, I looked to them so I could keep up with the up-and-coming trends. Between the four of us, two of us were always fighting at any given time. The fights never lasted long, though. We would snuff out our arguments to avoid being dealt any form of punishment that our parents might place on us.

What was nice about us all being born about two years apart was that I had a built-in best friend—my younger sister, Carly. We shared a room together for most of our childhood. We played together nearly every day. We got in trouble together and carried out our punishments side by side. We would get in trouble for being too wound up and would end up standing with our noses pressed in the corner of the room while our youngest sister danced around us singing the words "corner monkey" at my dad's request. Captain Carly and Commander Holly. It was etched into the wood behind the staircase that led to the basement—a memory that would remain there years later when the house was sold.

As the years went by, Carly began to make friends from school and in the neighborhood, causing us to spend less time together. I, on the other hand, struggled to form connections, finding myself alone more often than not. I turned to solitary activities like drawing or playing by myself to pass the time. I tried to find my place at school, but would end up on the playground digging through the rocks while the other kids played four square or kick ball.

Middle school didn't offer the fresh start I'd hoped for. I wanted to find friendship with someone who came from another school, who didn't know what a loner I truly was. The stark differences between elementary school and sixth grade left me feeling disconnected from my peers. Everyone seemed so different from me, like I was some sort of alien or outsider. For the next three years, my primary focus was to blend in and camouflage myself among the sea of unfamiliar faces.

The next year, I found a way to make friends in my math class. A handful of the cool kids were in class with me, even my grade school crush. They slacked off in class while I was attentive, and they would ask me to help them with their homework. They could probably see my desperation for interaction with them dripping from my chin. I was so eager to help that I ended up offering to do their homework for them. I would give them the answers the next day before class and they would write them out in their own handwriting. Tests? No problem. I would let my paper lie at the edge of my desk so the person next to me could see it, and they would pass the answers on to the others the same way. We even had a project at the end of the semester where we had to build a 3D shape using certain measurements. I showed up with my backpack full of different 3D shapes and handed them out to my new friends who, in return, paid me a few dollars. We never hung out outside of class. I would get a "hello" or "what's up?" in passing in the hallways, but that was it. It was worth the extra work, though.

I don't remember much about the next two years, probably because things at home were beginning to be a shitstorm. My parents got divorced, something that wasn't an option when you got married back then like it is today. It was viewed as an embarrassment to your family and was kept hush-hush. Expressing yourself was also viewed as shameful. That was why I learned to internalize the emotions and feelings I had during this time of my life.

During this time, my mother began to distance herself from our family outings. I didn't know that this was a sign that things were going wrong in my parents' marriage. It wasn't until I noticed that she was distancing herself from our home that I realized something was going on. It was about this time that my mom also started leaving the house more often, saying she had to run an errand or go to the grocery store. Four hours later, she would return empty-handed. We didn't think anything of it.

Mom was in nursing school, so she would sit at the dining room table and drown herself in homework. I would never say that she was neglectful to any of us; she was just focused on building a career for herself. But when I sit here and reflect on my childhood memories, I see that she wasn't present in many of them at all.

She took my youngest sister and me with her one day on one of her errands. We never actually went to any kind of store but stopped by her friend's apartment. She set us up on the computer to play around and went into the kitchen. I don't remember much about the place other than it was small and smelled musty. The computer wouldn't load whatever game she'd chosen for us to play, so I got up and went looking for my mom to help us. That's when I saw her and him in the kitchen.

Kissing. I ran back to the computer and started slamming all the buttons. I just sat there feeling a mix of anger, sadness, and confusion.

Do I tell my dad about this?

This internal struggle became my daily burden, especially when my mom would continue to go run her "errands." Dad caught on after a while. He followed her one day and watched her go into the mysterious apartment.

I'm not sure what happened after that, but the end result was divorce. I carried a heavy sense of guilt for a long time, always wondering if I'd said something, would things be different? I'll never know. I couldn't help but be mad at my mom for doing what she did. At the same time, I couldn't judge or understand her because I didn't know the state of the relationship between my dad and her. All I knew was that dad didn't want a divorce and was left heartbroken.

I always felt like the scapegoat for everything that went wrong from that point forward. It made me think that my mom knew I caught her kissing some guy that wasn't my dad, and that I'd revealed her secret to him. I couldn't seem to do anything right and was constantly getting into trouble around the house. Whether it was my room being a mess, not cleaning the bathroom well enough, or even just leaving a spoon in the sink, everything ended up being blamed on me, regardless of who was actually responsible.

My dad moved into a little apartment a few blocks away in order to stay near us. It had two bedrooms—one for him and then the one we would use. Despite there being four of us, only two beds would fit into our small bedroom. And his room was decorated like he was living in an African safari. A little unusual, but that was my dad. He lived close enough to my mom that we were able to ride our bikes there whenever we wanted and were still able to do our paper route on his weekends without any complications.

I made a few friends my freshman year in high school, but it wasn't until my sophomore year that I finally made a valuable connection with a popular girl. She let me tag along with her most days. She was stunning, with beautiful long, blond hair and bright blue eyes. She drove the nicest sports car that her dad's job as a dentist could afford. People always thought that she became friends with girls who were below her stature strictly so she could be the pretty one of the group. Maybe it was true, but at the time, I was just grateful to be included.

She showed me that if you wore miniskirts and makeup, then people would come to you to seek friendship. Sure, most of those new friends were males, but it seemed to work, funny enough. I would raid her closet when I went over to her house. She helped me pick out outfits and showed me how to apply makeup, since I had no idea how to put any of it on without looking like a drag queen. I became friends with her friend group, but eventually found myself meshed with the skater crowd—grungy-looking hoodlums out causing trouble, indulging in drinking alcohol, and smoking cigarettes and pot.

I began hanging out with the cool kids, waking up at 5:00 a.m. to go to the cafe before school on Friday mornings just to drink coffee and chain smoke cigarettes. After-school activities consisted of meeting up in a parking lot where everyone would show off their modified cars that Mommy and Daddy paid for, or riding up and down the Calumet/Lincolnway strip in hopes of running into some familiar faces.

I had three close girlfriends, and that was all the female companionship I could handle. For some reason, I always had an easier time being friends with the guys than the girls. I didn't mind getting dirty and I was always up to doing anything. Their girlfriends weren't fans of this, but it wasn't my fault that their boyfriend was ditching them to come hang out with me and the guys.

Many of the older guys were dating younger girls who were in my grade. Despite my desire to fit into their friend circle, I struggled to find anything in common with them. They all were caked in makeup and super girly, and I wasn't. I was more of a tomboy and related more to the guys than any of those girls.

This became a problem when my guy friends all graduated and I was stuck with all their girlfriends my junior year. I would get my stuff out of my locker and head straight to class, avoiding the hallways where I knew they congregated. I ended up becoming friendly with the girl next to my locker, who was training to be a bodybuilder. She would walk with me to class sometimes and if any of those prissy girls even looked at me wrong, she would flex right back, and they would leave me alone. Eventually, they backed off and navigating the hallways became less of a worry.

Chapter 1

I know what you're thinking: "Hey, isn't that the name of an old country song?"

Yes, it is—but the only similarity between that song and this book is the title. I wish my life panned out the way George Strait's did. Instead, all my exes reside in the great Midwest… the armpit of America… northwest Indiana. A place I don't really love to be, wishing I could hang my hat in Tennessee, or anywhere fucking else but here. Yet here I am.

Let me tell you something about this area. As much as I try to love it, I hate it. Being centrally located has its perks, though. I'm close to a majority of the things I need. I can drive twenty minutes and be at one of Lake Michigan's serene beaches. Craving the hustle and bustle of city life? I can hop over the state line and immerse myself in the vibrant energy of Chicago. And when I want to escape it all, it's just a quick hour-and-a-half drive to O'Hare International Airport, where I can jet off to any destination I want.

What don't I like? Where do I begin? For starters, you can't go anywhere looking like shit because no matter what time it is or where you go, you're guaranteed to run into someone you know. For some reason, if you're seen without makeup on or your hair done, everyone thinks you're dying. News flash: I *am* dying. My biological clock is ticking with each passing day. We're all going to end up on a mantel in someone's home or six feet under at some point, aren't we? Heaven forbid that you go out in public the way God intended you to look.

The worst thing of all is that there are people you don't even know who know more about you than you know about yourself. You're their topic of conversation. They spread gossip like wildfire regardless of who you are and how it affects the people involved. You can try and run away from this, but it will catch right up to you. Land right on your doorstep. Why don't you leave and move somewhere else?

Been there.

Done that.

Got sucked right back in.

That's what's so strange about this place. No matter how badly you want out, you find yourself right back where you started. I've known multiple people who have left, moved to the coast for a bit, and proudly showcased their new life far away from the clutches of this sinkhole town on social media. Then a year later, they're back, integrating into the fabric of local life, sipping the town tea at one of the local dive bars. Completely content being middle-aged, living in a shitty apartment above one of the restaurants downtown, shamelessly hitting on women at the bar who are the same age as their daughters. No ambition to change. No acting their age—which leads me to bring up the complete cesspool of a dating scene.

As a young adult, I couldn't wait to become an older adult, hoping that things would get better. But all I found out was that the older I got, the worse it became. In high school, it was as if everyone just passed each other around, swapping partners like trading cards. One week David is dating Jessica and Kevin is dating Liz. Then the next week, Jessica is dating Kevin and David is dating Liz. And so on and so forth. Since the dating pool was limited to those we went to school with, I envisioned that this wouldn't occur as we got older. That we would be able to branch out more. Boy, was I wrong! The only things that changed were the names and number of people involved. To gain a complete understanding of the relationships I experienced as an adult, it's helpful to reflect on the relationships I had during my childhood. The actions of my mother, father, and stepparents, whether they knew it or not, had a lasting detrimental effect on me for years to come. I acquired an immense fear of being rejected, leading me to seek approval and validation in various ways, morphing myself into whatever a particular person wanted me to be. When you pair this personality type with manipulative, narcissistic men, the resulting dynamic can be highly volatile.

Chapter 2

My mom didn't waste much time and ended up eloping with her new beau, Mark, somewhere down in Tennessee. My new stepdad was a real winner, let me tell you. At forty-something years old, he'd never been married and had no kids. Did he think marrying a woman with four teenage girls was going to be a walk in the park? He either couldn't or just wouldn't communicate with any of us. And when he did, it was never friendly.

Even at fifteen years of age, I always thought it was weird that one day he was just some guy and the next he was living in our house, and I had to obey his rules. For a guy who couldn't keep a steady job, he sure had a lot of rules. He even went as far as to stake his claim on certain groceries by writing his name on them in permanent marker—groceries that my mom had bought for everyone. And I didn't know until later that he didn't help Mom with paying the mortgage or contribute to paying any bills. He just lived there and did yard work and was an asshole. Needless to say, my sisters and I weren't his biggest fans.

He was always yelling at me to turn down the music that I'd put on my new three-piece stereo system that I got for my birthday. What was the point in having such a beautiful piece of machinery if I couldn't use it? I remember one day, I was minding my own business in my room, listening to the radio—kind of loudly, I'll admit. I had my door shut, hoping it didn't bother anyone. With my window open and the screen removed, I sat on the ledge wondering what it would feel like if I just jumped out of it. Was I suicidal? No, not at this time. I could faintly hear Mark's voice yelling through the door to turn down my music, so I did as I was told, only turning it down a couple of notches and then went back to my perch on the window ledge.

Apparently, I didn't turn it down enough, because the next thing I knew, Mark busted through my door. He lunged toward my stereo, proceeded to rip it from the wall, and hurled it at me as I sat on the windowsill. My thoughts of jumping almost became a reality, as I had to press myself against the window frame to keep my balance. Miraculously, I managed to avoid being hit. He stormed out of my room, slamming the door behind him so hard that it shook the entire house. I was in shock and scared. What in the hell just happened? And why in the fuck did he just do that? What if I actually fell out of the window? Would he have even helped me? My mom wasn't home, but I doubted if she would have done anything. I jumped up, locked my door, and curled up into the corner of my bed, sobbing.

I was uncharacteristically emotional the next day at school. I was upset about the previous day's events. I hated Mark. I hated my mom for being with him. I hated what he did to our family. Unfortunately, I was never good at showing any kind of emotion. All I knew how to do was cry. I'm happy, I cry. I'm mad, I cry. I'm sad… you guessed it, I cry. I was so full of anger that it was spilling over and presenting itself as silent tears rolling down my cheeks in the middle of class. My teacher saw me crying and took me out into the hall. She gave me a pass to go to the counselor's office, where I proceeded to tell some guy I'd never met before what had happened. At the time, I wasn't aware that they're obligated to call Child Protective Services any time something like this happens. And I didn't know they were called until I got home and got yelled at and grounded for it. So, I did what I did best and confined myself to my bedroom.

Things were as tense as they'd ever been between my mom and me. She did what she could to keep me in check so Mark wouldn't take it out on her. I think I was grounded over half the summer, which never made sense to me. If I was such a pain in the ass, why would you want me stuck in the house all day? I believe at some point she realized this same thing and decided to get more creative with my punishments.

At least once a week, I would come home to my clothes thrown across the front lawn by my mom, who had decided I'd disobeyed her in one way or another. I'd become so accustomed to this form of punishment that I didn't even bother to fold them when I placed them back into my drawers. I'd also gotten used to not really knowing what I'd done to deserve it. I would get calls at work yelling at me for leaving a spoon in the sink, of all things. I wasn't a messy kid; I just didn't see the point in some things. Like making my bed. Why did I need to make my bed if I was just going to get right back in it and mess it up again? I lost this battle every time. But a spoon? Christ almighty, a dirty spoon in the sink. Where dishes are washed. My bad.

My room was my little sanctuary, my safe place, even though

at times, it had been infiltrated with evil. I could always go to my room and run off to any imaginary place I wanted to. It was the only place I felt normal, surrounded by cut-out pictures from *Rolling Stone* and *Seventeen* magazines. My porcelain dolls I'd collected over the years watched over me from on top of my dresser. I would travel to a different world listening to music, pretending I was someone else with a different life until I fell asleep or was summoned to do a chore of some sort. I was functioning with a high level of anxiety and depression, but I didn't know or understand it.

I can't recall what I did, but I do remember the diabolical swipe of Mark's arm that knocked all of my porcelain dolls off the top of my dresser, sending them flying in the air. They crashed to the floor, leaving their beautiful, perfect faces cracked and shattered for an unknown reason. I should have and could have gotten upset or even cried. Those dolls were all gifts from my grandparents when I was younger, and a couple from my parents, if I remember correctly. I held onto them because they were special to me; they reminded me of a happier time. And yet there they were, scattered across my room, as broken as I was. I picked each one up to assess the damage.

It could have been worse, I guess. I got my glue out and got to work, putting together the porcelain puzzle as best I could. I gently placed them back in their stands on the top of my dresser. After I was done, I had to take action to protect what was important to me. I rearranged the furniture in my room. I didn't want my dolls close to the door, where they could be easily attacked again. My small body pushed and shoved my desk and dresser into different corners of the room. My dresser was on the back wall now, far from the door, and my dolls would be safe there. I took a step back and smiled. I was proud of myself. I refused to wallow in self-pity. I wouldn't place blame on anyone but myself for doing whatever I'd done to deserve this.

Chapter 3

By this time, my dad had married a woman with four kids of her own. Their family was... different. Maybe normal? They were church-going, God-fearing people with an incredible ability to kiss ass. We were White Trash by their standards. When I would compare our different families, it was like the Simpsons met the Brady Bunch. It was the best way to describe how different we were. My dad had moved into my stepmom's five-bedroom house overlooking a small lake located in a prestigious subdivision known to house most of the rich kids who went to my school. There was a pool in the back yard and beyond that, a path that took you down to the dock where a small speed boat and jet skis were tied up. Dotted throughout the house were candy dishes filled with M&Ms. The fridge was always stocked with Bagel Bites and Pepsi. It was a lifestyle unlike anything I'd ever been used to.

My stepmom was divorced as well. She was a stay-at-home mom while her ex worked as an engineer. I guess you could say that her job was entering sweepstakes. Like, hardcore entering sweepstakes. The boat and jet skis in the back yard? She won them. She'd won cars and trips and an array of other things too. She had a whole room dedicated to different color envelopes and paper stock. I never knew there was an actual science behind doing this kind of thing. I have to give it to her, she was good at it.

Her ex-husband had started a booming business that wasn't slowing down, and this was why when he told her he was leaving her for his twenty-four-year-old masseuse, he knew he was screwed. He walked out on them, leaving her the house and everything in it, and even paid her bills and mortgage as it was far less than what she would get if she decided to go after him. She had a pretty sweet deal, if you ask me.

She was a small, petite woman, soft-spoken and weighing no more than 100 pounds soaking wet. Despite her small stature, she had a loud, banshee-like laugh that carried through to every room in whatever building you were in. On the surface she was a sweet, older lady. It was unfortunate that beneath the facade, she was an awful, awful human being.

She couldn't stand sharing my dad's attention with my sisters and me. I was sure that she was brainwashing him behind closed doors, convincing him into thinking we only kept in touch with him because we wanted money. She would manipulate him into thinking we were the devil's spawn, driven by her deep-seated animosity toward my mom, especially during their ongoing court battles for child support. My stepmom would send my mom these nasty letters. I mean N-A-S-T-Y. She even sat in the courtroom during a hearing and threw such a conniption fit that the judge had her escorted out of the building. The judge felt so bad for my mom and what this lady was putting her through, so much so that later that evening, he sent pizza to our house.

Things continued to deteriorate for me at my mom's, forcing

my dad to consult with my stepmom about the possibility of me moving in with them. She reluctantly agreed, and I jumped at the chance. I packed my belongings in record time and settled into my new room. I even had my own phone in my room. A phone in my room. A *cordless* phone in my room. They didn't care how often I was on it. Or who I called. I even had the freedom to have friends over if I wanted, although I rarely took advantage of this privilege. I felt like things were starting to look up for me.

My dad helped me make an appointment at the Bureau of Motor Vehicles so I could finally get my driver's license. I'd already taken the written portion and was scheduled for the driving portion just before my permit was to expire. If I didn't take the driving test prior to the expiration, I would have to retake the exam to renew my permit, and then retake the driver's exam as well. I was scheduled to take it early on a Saturday morning.

My dad and I walked into the building together and headed up to the front desk to the sign in sheet. As I signed my name, the lady behind the counter asked what we were there for without taking her eyes off her computer screen.

"I have an appointment to take my driver's test."

The lady peered up over the rim of her glasses, looking at me, confused. "Barbara is on vacation this week. You'll have to reschedule."

I didn't know what to do at this point. My dad stood behind me, hands clasped behind his back, rocking back and forth on his feet.

"But I made an appointment. I have to take this test today. My permit is about to exp—"

I was cut off by my father, asking this woman if there was

a room or area where they could go and talk privately. She shook her head "no" in a dismissive manner, waving for the next person in line to approach the counter, unable to foresee what was coming next.

"Fine, have it your way."

At that point, my dad proceeded to give her a piece of his mind. When he was done with her, he continued walking down the row of employees sitting at their computers, bitching each and every one of them out, pointing and shaking his finger at them. By the time he got down to the last stall, the first lady had just hung up the phone.

"Sir, we got your daughter in at our Portage location. You can head straight there; they will take care of you."

I'd never in my life seen my dad that way. I didn't have to be mad at the situation; he was mad for me. I was half embarrassed and half proud of him for sticking up for me like that. We left and made the drive over to the other location, about twenty minutes away.

My dad held the door open for me as we passed through the main lobby. It was busy here, but that didn't matter. It was as if Moses had reached his arms out and parted the Red Sea. The crowd of people parted, revealing a path right up to the front desk, where a man stood smiling and gesturing to us to come forward.

"Mr. Wells, we're so glad you made it. And this must be Holly! Are you ready to take your driver's test?"

The man appeared slightly nervous but held himself together well. I couldn't believe what was happening. We had celebrity status at the license branch. I followed him out to the car and we began my test. We tested the turn signals first, then we put the car in reverse, slowly inching my way out of the parking space.

I was back inside two minutes later. These people were scared shitless that my dad would cause another scene, so much so that my test drive entailed circling the parking lot and parking back in the same spot. No parallel parking that I had practiced over and over. No highway driving. I never left the parking lot. I passed with flying colors.

Chapter 4

It was around this time when the differences between myself and my step family started to become apparent. My stepmom would make dinner, and if you didn't praise her on how good it was, she would get upset. I always said please and thank you, thinking that was enough. I would clear my plate, and to me that was the ultimate compliment. I would rinse my dish and put it in the dishwasher (yes, a dishwasher, thank sweet baby Jesus). But it wasn't enough. She would send my dad to come talk with me about it. I could tell that he was embarrassed having to do so. I would just say that I would try to do better next time.

I began to notice signs that my stepmom didn't like the attention Dad gave me. A casual conversation with my dad during dinner turned into her interjecting to tell one of her stories. If I dared to speak up, I was cut off with her banshee laugh, redirecting the attention back to her. She wanted his attention at all times. To her, I was competition, and she was determined to be the winner in her one-sided game. I could feel her gaze drilling into me whenever we were in the same room, making me feel incredibly uneasy. Eventually, her efforts to make me feel unwanted were successful. I found myself living back at Mom's house, finding ways to get away from my real life.

My stepmom finally resorted to her most extreme tactic and threatened my dad with divorce if he didn't do as she said. She wanted nothing to do with us and didn't want my dad to have anything to do with us either. Her cancerous opinions of us had finally overtaken my dad's judgment, and he succumbed to her demands. He dialed the number to my mom's house and waited for us to pick up on the other end. He said he wanted to talk to all of us, so two of us ran upstairs to the phone in Mom's bedroom and the other two listened on the kitchen phone. He proceeded to suggest that our interactions with him were solely motivated by financial gain, stating that he now had a new family and believed it would be best for him to step out of the picture. We all sat there, silent, processing the weight of his words.

I don't know what was worse: hearing him say this or the fact that we could all hear our stepmom in the background telling him what to say. I heard the phone slam upstairs and within seconds, I was standing by myself with the phone pressed hard against my ear. It was just him and me on the line. I couldn't believe what he was saying and that he would let this woman dictate his life like this. Where was the dad who stood up for me at the license branch? Grow some balls, Dad! Even though he was saying all this stuff to us, I couldn't help but feel bad for him. He never wanted to divorce my mom, and I knew he didn't want to go through that again. So instead of lashing out, I found myself expressing the unspoken thoughts that he and I both shared.

"Okay, Dad. I'll see you when she dies," I said and hung up.

This experience messed me up more than I thought it would,

and I wouldn't realize it until I hit different periods throughout my life. I loved my dad. I loved it when he lived in the apartment and it was just us and him. We shared special moments like fishing and swing dancing lessons at the museum in Chicago. The time and effort he spent with us didn't go unnoticed. How did he go from my favorite parent to this seemingly weak man? It was hard to wrap my mind around what was going on.

When I reflect on all of this in the long run, I realize how much alike he and I were. Our willingness to make our significant other happy outweighed our own happiness. When I look back at the things I went through or the things I put myself through, I can see now how what he did impacted my decision-making in every past relationship I found myself in.

I would like to say I made progress in the relationships I had as I got older. The one thing that seems to be a constant is my poor choice in men. My problem is that I see good in everyone. I can see their potential even if they can't. No one is perfect; at least I admit it. Yet I hold onto the belief that two imperfect people can come together and create something beautiful. Life itself isn't perfect and if you claim it to be, then you're one of those people who have a lot to hide.

That's probably why I can never seem to make the transition from girlfriend to wife. I know I'm not perfect, and I'm willing to work on that. My exes? Well, good Lord, wouldn't you know they've never done anything wrong in their lives? They shit gold, piss rainbows, and vomit sunshine. Okay, maybe a few of them weren't *that* bad, but they were pretty darn close.

I've spent a lot of time bettering myself over the years, and for someone to be completely content with their miserable self just doesn't sit well with me. We all have the capability to become better versions of ourselves; it's an essential part of being human. We're ever-evolving creatures. If you aren't spending part of your life learning from the mistakes you've made, then what are you even doing here?

Chapter 5

My very first boyfriend lasted all of twenty-four hours—and that includes over night when I was sleeping. It was in my second year of the third grade. I was held back due to my poor grades in math and what I later came to find out was my lack of social skills.

My crush, who lived a few blocks away, was one of the coolest kids in the class. I think the only reason we were friends was because he lived in the neighborhood. I did anything I could to hang around with him. His dad worked for the local newspaper, so he spent every day after school delivering papers. He would usually stop by our house and ask if I could help him finish the last half of the route. He never knew that every day I was waiting for him by the door with my shoes on, hoping he would show up. There were even times I would finish the route off alone while he stayed at our house watching MTV and having a snack.

I never expected what happened during one of our nightly summer neighborhood campouts. We were all sitting around playing cards, and he walked up to me and asked me out. Everyone there was giggling, waiting for my response. I never liked being the center of attention. I could feel myself getting hot with anxiety. I'm sure my face, burning with embarrassment, reflected every shade of red on the color spectrum. I was fumbling, putting the three letters together in my head and trying to remember how to say the word "yes," but finally, I was able to blurt it out. Almost immediately after, I ran home and locked myself in my room. I saw him a few days later, and we both just pretended like it never happened. But hey, that still counts as my first boyfriend, right?

My first high school boyfriend didn't last very long either. Aaron was quiet and soft spoken with fair skin, ice blue eyes, and white-blond hair. He was a little on the grungy side but this was the '90s, so it was the way to be at the time. Occasionally, I would see him around town skateboarding with his friends, taking breaks to smoke cigarettes or to show off a new trick one of them had mastered. During lunch one day, I found out he had a crush on me. He and his group of friends sat at the table next to mine, and eventually, we all started sitting at the same table.

Aaron was just as shy as me. Putting two shy people together doesn't make for the greatest conversation. We barely talked to each other, but we talked enough to become a couple. With him, I had built-in friends. And his friends had cars. I became one of their regular passengers to and from school and didn't have to rely on my sister or her friends to take me home.

One day on the ride home from school, my friend Katie came to the realization that she'd never seen Aaron and me kiss. I'd never really kissed anyone and went into panic mode. I awkwardly laughed it off and made up some sort of excuse, but Katie being Katie began to lay on the pressure all the way up until we pulled up to my house. Nervously, I looked at Aaron sitting next to me, desperately trying to figure my way out of this. I did the only thing I could come up with. I leaned in and I politely gave him a kiss on the cheek, hurried out of the car, and went inside.

Whew!

That was a close one!

A few weeks later, things between Aaron and me fizzled out. We remained friends, but my issue really was that I didn't know how to date someone. I wasn't ready for the pressures of a relationship. I never really knew what it meant to care for or be on an intimate level with someone. And I sure as hell didn't know how to express any kind of emotion or talk about... ewww... feelings.

Now, I cannot tell the story about my first love, Bryan, without talking about Vinny first. This is where I believe I got stuck on a "type." The tall, dark, and handsome syndrome is *real*, folks! Vinny was just that. And Italian.

Vinny was a friend of my older sister's. They worked together at a pizza place, and he was friends with her boyfriend and other friends from work too. The exact moment we met is a bit fuzzy; perhaps it was one of the times when my group of friends intermixed with my sister's group of friends. He had connections with some of my friends in the car club too, since he also owned a fast car. When Vinny and I started dating, it royally pissed my sister off.

How dare I have the same friends as her?

How dare I listen to the same music as her?

How dare I dress the same as her?

I found this quite ironic given that a significant portion of my wardrobe consisted of hand-me-downs from her. Typical older sister stuff, I guess.

Despite being more reserved, she had genuine friendships.

Her group of friends were the kind they base movies on. Now, I'm not bashing my older sister. In fact, she did something that I truly admire her for. There was a time in high school when a rumor was going around about me messing around with one of the football players. When she got wind of it, she walked up to him in the hallway, got right in his face, and called him out for lying. It was a bold move, one that I never expected from her. As much as we didn't get along at times, her doing that showed me that she actually did care about me. And I thank her for that.

When she found out I was dating Vinny, she wasn't exactly thrilled. Now I would be hanging around her and her friends and hindering her life. In actuality, there were very few times when our paths crossed. So, it wasn't all that bad. Surprisingly, her friends were all very nice to me. I was actually kind of excited to get to know my sister on a friend level. Our relationship growing up wasn't particularly strong and honestly, it wasn't until we were older that we started to develop a more meaningful bond as sisters.

My relationship with Vinny was brief and ended abruptly. I was seventeen when we dated, and out of all of my friends or people I knew, I was the only virgin among them. I liked Vinny enough to decide that it was time for me to join the "not a virgin anymore" club. I made the decision to just get it over with. It wasn't based on whether I loved him or not, because I didn't.

Not even close.

My first time was nothing to write home about. I think he was scared that he was going to break me or something. He kept asking me questions like if I was okay or was I sure I wanted to do this. Despite his concern, I was glad I'd gotten it done and over with. I honestly didn't see what the big deal was. It wasn't very comfortable or enjoyable. So why was everyone so obsessed with doing it all the time? I didn't get it. Maybe I was doing something wrong; that wouldn't have surprised me. After all, I had no idea what I was doing in the first place. I'd hoped that doing this would make me like him more but instead, it just made me feel more awkward.

I often hung out with my new friend Natalie, who was well acquainted with everyone I seemed to find myself around. She'd dated a guy named Justin, but they'd recently broken up and she was doing all she could to win him back. They were still friendly to each other, but her desperation was off-putting. Consequently, I began to hang out with other people when Natalie wasn't able to join us. This allowed me to make friends with some of the other members in the group.

I found myself hanging out with Justin and a few of the other guys more often than not. They were a lot of fun, always up to something, and it was easy for me to feel comfortable around them. We would all meet up in the parking lot until the cops showed up and made us leave. At that point, we would head to Jake's house. His mom had a decent-sized property, with a large pole barn in the back that had a loft they'd turned into a hangout spot. This was where we would partake in underage drinking and partying all night. His mom didn't seem to care or know exactly what was going on in her back yard. At least we weren't driving around drinking and doing stupid shit that would get us thrown in jail. We confined that to the pole barn.

Justin was cool, a real James Dean of our generation: hand-some, ruthless, and reckless. He had a presence that com-manded respect, and I wasn't really sure why. When he and I hung out one-on-one, I would see glimpses of the kind and gentle person he hid and a twisted sense of humor, which I found amusing. I always wondered if he felt bad for me and that was why he was my friend. Or maybe that was his way of passive aggressively pissing Natalie off. It was never anything more than friendship. He would bitch about Natalie acting like a psycho, and I would try to offer insight as to why she was behaving that way.

Natalie had asked if I would accompany her to visit Justin's brother Bryan, who had just gotten out of jail. Even though she was no longer dating him, she was still friends with his family. I always thought she remained friends with Justin's brother as a ploy to try to win him back. I'll circle back to this thought later. Anyway, we headed to his mom's house, where I was first introduced to Bryan.

Bryan's reputation preceded him. Any time anyone mentioned his name, everyone knew who he was. He'd caused so much trouble around town and was considered the ultimate bad boy, which gained him a strange popularity among the younger girls. He thought his popularity stemmed from his stepdad's wealth and living in a big ass house. This allowed him to have the nice cars and motorcycles that made him "cool."

Despite Bryan's troubled past and involvement in criminal activities, meeting him in person was a stark contrast to my expectations. I was expecting to see some hardened, strung-out criminal like in the movies and TV shows. Instead, I met this charming, dark-haired, skinny kid who had a warped sense of humor and a keen intellect. Being incarcerated had forced him to stay clean, so he was on the road to recovery and had the support from friends and family to do so. Despite his past mistakes, you could see a glimmer of hope for a better future radiating from him.

Natalie and I were only a few of the many visitors he had, mostly girls from my grade. Later, I found out that he'd started dating one of them right before he was sent to jail. I guess they communicated through letters and collect calls. I think she even took the time to go visit him while he was in the slammer.

I was trying my best to find other things to do so I didn't have to see Vinny. My friends and I would hang out with Bryan every now and then through the next couple of weeks, either at his mom's house or at his stepdad's house. I struggled to engage in conversation with him at first.

We came from two different worlds. After all, I was just some shy, Goody Two-shoes, completely basic girl with nothing to offer. A few times, I noticed that he was making an effort to include me in the conversation. I was the only one who could offer any intelligent input on whatever topic was being talked about. Not that those other girls were dumb, but I guess I just had more of the kind of intellect that intrigued him. I also wasn't a super bitch like some of them. They were constantly fighting with someone or talking shit about their most recent rival. I may have had my opinions on some people, but I kept them to myself.

Natalie would call me, saying Bryan wanted to hang out with us. This became a more frequent occurrence, and I didn't mind. It was interesting seeing his brain in action. I knew he was a criminal, but honestly, his thought process behind it all was pretty amazing. He had a different way of viewing things, one that I could appreciate. I found myself over at his house more often than not. I couldn't help but feel some sort of connection forming between him and me.

As a bunch of us were about to leave, Bryan pulled me into the bathroom and locked the door behind us. And he kissed me. He kissed me in a way that I'd never been kissed before and I just melted. It was sweet. It was passionate. I felt like I was being lifted off the floor by all the butterflies in my stomach.

It was a whirlwind of emotions and confusion. I mean, I had a boyfriend I was supposed to be in love with. And he had a girlfriend who had been loyal to him while he was in jail… What were we doing?! I had my first real boyfriend and here I was cheating on him. And not only with a kiss. That one kiss spiraled into the whole shebang. Lines were crossed and boundaries were blurred. I let it happen. With one bathroom rendezvous, I'd silently broken up with Vinny, and Bryan had silently broken up with What's-her-name.

And now? I was Bryan's girlfriend and he was my boyfriend. I didn't even have the decency to tell Vinny about it either. He found out from Bryan's ex-girlfriend. He called me, crying and yelling. I didn't know what to do or say so I hung up on him. I felt horrible for what I'd done to Vinny. Years down the road, I even gave him a sloppy, drunken apology.

I was surprised to find out that as much as good girls like bad guys, bad guys like good girls. And Bryan and I were just that. My innocence had a gravitational pull on him, and I couldn't help but be attracted to the excitement and danger of being with him. He was unlike anyone I'd ever known. I could tell there was a good person hiding behind the bad boy persona. He just needed the right person to help him see that. For some naive reason, I thought I could be that person.

Chapter 6

The time I used to spend on the phone with my friends turned into countless calls with Bryan, even if we weren't actively talking. I spent most of my lunch breaks at school on the pay phone in the lobby. He wanted me to call every day, mostly to make sure that I wasn't talking to any other guys. In the evening I would call from home, and we would stay on the phone until late at night. When I wanted to hang up, he would get pissed, accusing me of not loving him because I would rather go to bed than talk to him. Many nights, I fell asleep on the kitchen floor with the phone in my hand, just to avoid upsetting him, even though he'd dozed off himself. He had a tight grip on me. I was his puppet, obedient to his every demand. I loved him and my world revolved around him. And the fact that my mom absolutely hated him made him perfect.

I would lie and say I was staying the night at a friend's house so I could spend the night with him every chance I could. I thought his mom was so cool for letting him have sleepovers with the opposite sex. There seemed to be no real rules in their house, besides doing what you were told when asked. We stayed up all night talking until the early hours of the morning, falling asleep to the glow of the TV. One morning, we were awakened by the ring of his cell phone. It was his stepdad, George.

"Hey… hey, Bryan… Hey… guess what…"

He spoke so loudly I could hear every word the man was saying without Bryan having to put him on speaker. There was an unsettling undertone in his voice, almost sadistic in nature.

Bryan rubbed the sleep out of his eyes and wearily answered. "What do you want?"

"Hey… Where was your girlfriend last night?"

We looked at each other, confused. He knew I was with him all night. There was no way I'd had a chance to sneak out and leave him. Why would I do that in the first place? I'd already lied to my mom in order to be able to be here with him.

Before Bryan could even respond, George began laughing. "Well, I know where she was… She was with me!"

He let out a demonic laugh, so loud, so boisterous. Bryan let out an exasperated sigh as he clenched his jaw. Through pursed lips, he responded with a solid, "Fuck you," before hanging up.

I looked at Bryan, eyebrows raised, unable to hide the look of sheer confusion on my face. What the fuck just happened? Did his stepdad really just call to say that to him? Was he insinuating that he was fucking around with me behind Bryan's back? What kind of parent does that? I compared how different our parents were while processing what I'd just heard. Bryan had hinted at his stepdad's toxic behavior before, but this blatant display of malice was beyond anything I'd ever expected. Bryan had given me a few examples of what his stepdad put him through, but never the full extent of it.

George always had a way of casting doubt on Bryan's life,

even through adulthood. He was the dark cloud, there to ruin his sunny day. With one phone call, George had poisoned our perfect relationship. Bryan began to keep a closer eye on me, becoming more controlling over what I did and who I talked to. He didn't believe George, no, but a bug had been placed in his ear that I was up to no good.

My mom was fed up with the chaos Bryan brought into our lives, resorting to taking drastic measures to limit our communication. Bryan had a car and no rules. I would get home from school some days, go to grab the phone and dial his phone number, just to realize that the phone cord was missing. Sometimes, the phone itself was taken right off the wall. I was left isolated, with no way to communicate with anyone, let alone Bryan. When Mom would finally put the phone back, I would have to sneak phone calls. I would make sure she was asleep or occupied when I dialed a number and kept the conversations short, so I didn't get in trouble again.

Taking the phone off the wall was just one thing my mom was willing to do to put a wedge between Bryan and me. On top of being grounded all the time, I wasn't allowed to keep my door shut. I never listened to this. I thought it was silly that I couldn't have some privacy whether I was grounded or not. So, it was no shock to me that my doorknob was missing out of the blue one day. So much for shutting my door. I didn't complain or throw a fit about it, and I didn't know if one was anticipated. Instead, I put a sock in the hole where my doorknob had been and propped something against it to keep it semi closed when I needed space from what I was surrounded with. I thought once I was ungrounded, the doorknob would magically appear as suddenly as it had disappeared, but it never happened.

Either way, I went on with my life and didn't let it get to me.

I got it back at Christmas in the year 2000. Every Christmas, each of my sisters and I got one big gift and a handful of small ones. I received my big gift last. I was handed a small gift bag filled with tissue paper and the handles tied together with a curly ribbon. It had some weight to it, so I was having a hard time guessing what it could be. I set the bag in my lap and pulled the tissue out, only to see my doorknob at the bottom. I just stared at it. I don't know what made me angrier: the fact that this was my gift, or the laughter that came along with it. This moment solidified my hatred for being at home. I was bound and determined to find a way out from this point forward.

I devoted myself entirely to Bryan, eager to show him how much I cared about him, although I wasn't sure how. I figured doing whatever he asked of me was a good start. I fulfilled his every request and this, of course, made him happy. He didn't have to worry about who I was with, what I was doing, or if I was talking to any boys who weren't him. In return, he would be my boyfriend, and that's what I wanted more than anything. I began to separate myself from my family and friends, prioritizing my time with him and his unpredictable circle of friends.

Shit was really hitting the fan at home, so the day I turned eighteen, and I mean down to the second, I had my bags packed, sitting on the porch waiting for Bryan to pick me up. Just to be an asshole, I sat there smoking a cigarette when my mom pulled in the driveway. She walked up to me and handed me a small gift, wished me a "happy birthday," and walked inside. As Bryan pulled up, I threw the gift into one of my bags unopened and loaded them into his car.

I had mixed emotions on the drive to his mom's house. I was

sad and proud of myself for growing a set, and also worried that his mom would tell me to get the hell out of her house and go home. This was my way out and if it didn't work out, I didn't know what I was going to do. We pulled up to his house and my nerves set in. I'd never really been away from home before; this was totally out of character for me. We walked into the garage and as Bryan opened the door, his mom and three sisters were there with a cake with eighteen candles on it singing "Happy Birthday" to me. His mom even had a gift for me: an emerald ring, my birthstone. I still have it to this day. I didn't know it, but Bryan had already talked to his mom about me moving in with them, and she was happy to have me. I could have cried, and I think I did. A family that actually wanted me there. It was a feeling I hadn't had in a long time.

I would wake up and get ready for school. Since Bryan had already graduated, he would take me there, or sometimes I would hitch a ride with his younger brother, Gabe, who was in my grade. Bryan insisted that I continue to call him on my lunch break, so most of my lunch time was spent at the pay phones in the hallway eating a candy bar. When I returned home, he would question me about any interactions I had with boys and grill me on my day's events. He was consumed with jealousy of the unknown and hated the idea of another guy potentially having my attention. Regardless of my reassurance, he still viewed anyone with a penis as a potential risk to our relationship.

The high school I went to was big, and drugs were beginning to become quite a problem. Randomly, the school would bring in police dogs to sniff out the lockers, checking for contraband. This time when they were brought in, the dogs stopped at my locker, detecting my Camel Light cigarettes. I was summoned to the principal's office, where my guidance counselor and principal sat, legs crossed and arms folded.

"Care to explain where these came from?" the principal asked.

"The gas station. I'm eighteen and legally allowed to have them."

"Cigarettes are not allowed on school property. If we catch you with them again, you will have to pay the consequences."

I'd never been in trouble in school. Besides detention for being tardy on a few occasions, I'd always obeyed the rules. I maintained good grades and my teachers seemed to like me. I was nervous, with this being the first time I'd gotten in trouble out of all the years I'd been in school. Given my experience with my family, I was prepared to stand my ground, perhaps even talk back for once. I was calculating exactly how I would answer their question when they brought up a completely different subject.

"I hear you're dating Mr. Galanis… See him picking you up after school…"

I just sat there wondering what this had to do with the pack of smokes they'd found in my purse.

"That kid is nothing but trouble. And you seem like a decent student with a good head on your shoulders. We'd hate to see you take the same path he has."

I remained seated, staring at them. Bryan and I had gotten into a fight the day prior. He was pissed that I didn't call him at exactly 11:15 when my lunch started and immediately accused me of talking to another guy. His jealousy and controlling behavior were coming to a head, and all I wanted was to prove my love to him and make him happy.

"I don't see what that has to do with anything. Can I go

now?"

"Mr. Galanis is no longer allowed on school property. Not to pick you up. Not to drop you off. If we see him here again, you are looking at suspension."

I didn't react well to this threat. Since leaving home, I'd grown more courageous, and I could feel it brewing inside me at this moment. What had he done to this school that was so bad he couldn't even be in the parking lot? What had I done to deserve this? My mind raced through my options. I had nothing keeping me there, and that was what they failed to see. The words that came out of my mouth next came as a shock to everyone in the room, including myself.

"In that case, I'd like to sign myself out of school."

To hell with the cigarettes! They made it very clear that this was far bigger than that. I had six weeks left of my junior year. All of my friends had already graduated, and the girls in my classes still all hated me. The tables had turned, and I held the power in the room. After seeing the mistake they'd made, the backpedaling began. They told me I was making a huge mistake; they didn't want me to go. I'd come this far, and I only had one year left. At that point, I didn't care. My sole focus was proving to Bryan how much I loved him. Now we could be together all the time, and he could see that I was faithful to him. I couldn't get out of there fast enough.

I stood up and snatched my purse and cigarettes off the desk, avoiding the disappointed looks being thrown in my direction. Once I got out of the office and into the hallway, I let out a deep breath.

What in the hell did I just do?

I made my way down to my locker to grab my backpack, leaving behind all my books and everything else. Not my problem anymore. I had to go back to the office a few days later to sign the papers; if there was anything else I needed, I could grab it then. I had to get out of that hell hole as soon as possible before the weight of my decision fully sank in.

I stood outside the back doors, waiting for the bell to ring to dismiss the students. Bryan would be there any minute to pick me up. I wondered if the principal was watching me. I hoped he was, just to give him one final kick in the ass.

Bryan pulled up and made his own parking spot in front of the handicap spot. I ran to the car and jumped in. I couldn't wait to tell him the news. He was the most surprised out of everyone at what I'd done. Part of the reason he liked me was because I was smart. After all, he admired my intelligence, and quitting school wasn't exactly the smartest move. I could sense a brief spell of disappointment, but at the end of the day, it was my decision and he supported it. Besides, now he could monitor my every move, so he became okay with it pretty quick.

It took them two days to write up the documents I needed to sign. I walked into the office with my head held high and a stern look on my face, trying to mask my inner uncertainty. A few of my teachers were present in an attempt to talk me out of quitting. I took a seat across from the principal and reached for the pen sitting on top of the papers. I looked at him dead in the eyes after setting the pen down, not saying a word.

"Holly, are you sure you want to do this? This is your last chance."

"I have to leave. Bryan is outside waiting for me."

I rose out of my seat and turned toward the door, leaving my high school days behind. To this day, my family thinks I was expelled for having cigarettes.

Chapter 7

I did my best to encourage Bryan to create a better version of himself. I helped him find work in a warehouse for a liquidation company that was closing down a furniture store in town. I joined him soon after, working in the office filing papers as a cashier. Once the store in our town officially closed, we followed the same company to South Bend, Indiana to close another. We lived out of a motel room where other coworkers of ours stayed. It was a different way of life, but it was cheap and gave us a roof over our heads. At the time, it was all we needed.

Every now and then I would get a phone call at my desk from my mom.

"Holly? Are you okay? Are you pregnant?"

Half of the time, I would hang up without answering. The other half, I would tell her to leave me alone and then hang up. I was done with that chapter of my life. I wanted to forget all the bullshit I'd gone through. I was happy and in love, and we were making it all on our own with no one's help. I didn't need her—or anyone, for that matter. All I needed was Bryan. And all he needed was me.

We worked seven days a week, spending the weekends

driving around posting those "store closing" signs on the street corners for extra cash. I was happy that Bryan seemed to have found a job he was good at; one that kept him busy and away from the trouble that always seemed to find him.

This kind of job, though, drew in a certain kind of individual. Most of the other guys working in the warehouse were just like Bryan: former criminals, criminals, and future criminals. They were either trying to make a quick buck so they could score their next fix, or they needed a legitimate job and steady flow of income in order to prove they had a way to make their child support payments to their multiple baby mommas without having to sell drugs.

It didn't take long for Bryan to make friends with these guys. Most of them came from rough areas where access to street drugs never posed a problem. At first, he just smoked pot with them after work but not long afterward, this turned into dabbling with the heavier stuff. He did a good job of hiding it from me for quite a while. I was oblivious to that world but would learn the signs of substance abuse as time went on.

We got word that our job in South Bend was wrapping up. The company wanted us to stay on and transfer to the next job, either somewhere in Florida or Arlington, Virginia. I'd hoped for the Florida job since winter was right around the corner. As luck would have it, we got the last pick of places to go, so Arlington it was. While disappointed, I still embraced the opportunity for a fresh start and looked forward to a new adventure.

I had an odd feeling throughout the final weeks of our job that I couldn't put my finger on, but I did my best to shrug it off. There were multiple times where I couldn't ignore the recurrence of families with small babies that flooded the showroom. Like it was "bring your baby to the furniture store" day. Everywhere I went, every corner I turned, I encountered a baby. Or babies. Not small children, but tiny, pink-faced babies. I knew deep down that God was trying to tell me something. During my lunch break, I finally decided to figure out what was going on once and for all. I went to the drug store and picked up a pregnancy test, hiding it in the bottom of my purse.

That Friday evening, we headed back to Valparaiso to spend the weekend at Bryan's mom's house. I never mentioned to Bryan the inkling feeling I had about being pregnant; after all, I had no idea if I was or not. Once we got to his mom's house, we settled in and made ourselves at home. Bryan headed down to his room to play video games with his younger sister. Now seemed like the perfect time for me to go take the test.

I locked myself in the bathroom, put the toilet seat down, and sat down. I carefully peeled back the cardboard edges of the box, worried that if I mishandled anything, it would lead to a false reading. I gingerly pulled the contents out and placed them on the sink. The directions were neatly folded into a little packet, and the test itself was in a separate package. I unfolded the directions, smoothing them in my lap so it was easier to read.

This can't be all that hard... right?

I read the directions over and over to make sure I didn't make any mistakes. I couldn't afford any mistakes.

Okay.

Pee on a stick, put the cover on, set it down as flat as possible. And wait.

Two pink lines: you're pregnant. One pink line: you're not. It seemed simple enough.

My kit came with two tests, so if I felt like I did it wrong the first time, at least I could try it again to make sure.

Here goes nothin'.

I set the test on the counter after I put the cover on and waited for what seemed like forever. I bent down to eye level, making sure it wasn't tilted more to one side, ensuring it was as level as possible. I began pacing back and forth, staring at the little window that determined my future. The urine slowly crept across the window, revealing nothing at first.

But... wait. I see a line.

Is it one line? I can't tell, it's too faint!

Wait, wait... Is that... a second line?

Oh no... had I moved the test and fucked it all up? I knew it said to wait fifteen minutes, but I could see it now! I must have messed something up. Of course I did! The two faint pink lines became more prominent as I sat back on the toilet to take the other test, making a meticulous effort to get things right this time.

I got a bad test. Yeah, that's it. It happens. No big deal. That's why I got the box with two tests in it, just for this reason.

I gently placed the second test right next to the first. I sat on the floor, rubbing my temples with my fingers. I promised to wait the entire fifteen minutes before looking at the results. I sat there... waiting... my heart racing... Was it warm in there or was it just me? Why the fuck was fifteen minutes taking so damn long? I stood up, keeping my eyes closed, trying to manifest one pink line. I opened my eyes and there they were.

Two solid pink lines.

Fuck. I'm pregnant...

I felt conflicted. I'd always pictured this moment as a happy one. I wanted a family of my own, but not at eighteen years old!

I was overcome with uncertainty and then fear. The reality of it all was hitting me in the confines of this small bathroom. How was I supposed to take care of a baby when I could barely take care of myself? I was just a fucked-up kid, despite my pleas to be seen as an adult. I wanted all the perks that came along with adulthood but none of the responsibility. I had all of these questions and scenarios swimming through my head, and I became angry.

IDIOT.

YOU FUCKING IDIOT!

How could I let this happen?

Maybe... wait... maybe I didn't do anything wrong...

It was HIM.

HE DID THIS! IT'S ALL HIS FAULT!

I was a good kid, never got into any real trouble my entire life! And now this? Oh, was I mad. I was beyond mad. I was furious at him.

I grabbed both of the tests with my fists and stormed out of the bathroom, letting the door hit the wall behind me. I headed down the stairs to Byran's room, pushing through before I came to a halt. I stood there for a few long seconds. He and his sister were staring intently at the TV, methodologically pushing buttons on the controllers, bickering back and forth.

How do I even bring this up? "Hey, Bryan, I'm pregnant," or "Guess what, Bryan? You got me knocked up." Yeah, either of those will work.

"Hey, Bryan..."

He acknowledged me with a quick glance back in my direction to not mess his game up. I went to say those exact words, but instead threw my arm back and whipped the tests right at his head.

"YOU MOTHER FUCKER!"

He ducked down as the pieces of plastic struck him, unaware of what they were and clueless as to what was going on. By the time he looked up, I'd already stormed out of the room, grabbing my purse on the way.

I marched out of the house into the darkness of the night. I intended on making the long hike back to my mom's place to tell her she'd been right all along. I was crying and cursing Bryan the whole way down the block when I heard hurried footsteps behind me. It was him. He was laughing.

He ran in front of me and stopped me in my tracks, still chuckling.

"What's the matter? Why are you mad at me? Are we really gonna have a baby?"

I was so confused by his reaction… Was he actually happy about this? Did he not understand what having a baby entailed and all the things that went along with taking care of a child for the next eighteen years? I had so many things I wanted to say, and to yell, but the only thing I could muster were whimpers and sobs. Instead of him walking me back to the house, we just kept walking. And talking. About what to do, how we were going to do this, when we should tell our parents.

Our parents.

Shit.

How in the hell was I going to tell my mom that she'd been right? That I wasn't okay and that I was, in fact, pregnant. I couldn't tell her—not now, anyway—so I set that task on the back burner and focused on the immediate future.

Over the next few days, the weight of the situation became heavy for both of us. Bryan approached the subject casually, suggesting that maybe I should get an abortion. The thought had never occurred to me. It was something I hadn't considered, mostly because it was something I would never do. I dismissed the idea, while knowing that there was another option out there lingered in the back of my head. It began to become an everyday suggestion from him, and then finally a demand, without ever demanding it.

He was testing me, trying to see how far I would go with it, presenting it in a way that made it seem like it was my idea. He made it clear that while the decision ultimately rested with me, he wasn't sure how he would feel about me if I actually followed through with it. He didn't know if he could love me knowing that I willingly put an end to the life of our child. At this same time, he reached into his pocket and withdrew our debit card. Flipped the piece of plastic in his hands, inspecting it… He gently pressed it onto the TV stand, sliding it with his fingers in my direction. He always had a way of getting what he wanted without ever flat out asking for it. He could manipulate words to make me think I was in control of the situation when in reality, he was playing me like a pawn in his game.

* * *

I sat in the parking lot of Planned Parenthood. It was 9:00 a.m. My appointment was in fifteen minutes. I just sat there, watching the clock on the radio ticking away, trying to stop time.

What am I doing here? Can I really go through with this? The tears welled up in my eyes. I was at a crossroads, and each road took me down a completely different path. I could go in there, follow through with this, and pretend like it never happened. I would be sent straight to hell, but I planned on living a long life, so I had time to make good with God.

Or…

I could live up to the consequences of my actions and raise this baby the best I knew how, with a possible chance of walking through the heavenly gates. I went through scenario after scenario in my adolescent, inexperienced head. Before I knew it, it was 9:15. I clenched the steering wheel with both hands before turning the key in the ignition to the Off position. I opened the car door and stepped outside, taking a deep breath. I could do this. I reached up to wipe my running mascara off my cheeks and what was left of the tears from my eyes. I gently pushed the car door shut behind me and made my way up the sidewalk.

Chapter 8

I sat on the edge of our cheap motel room bed sobbing, the pressure in my head so strong I thought it was going to explode. I'd walked all the way up to the entrance of Planned Parenthood only to turn around and run back to my car. I couldn't do it. I didn't have the heart to. I drove back to our makeshift home in a haze, contemplating my life and the decision I'd just made. I would raise this child on my own if it came down to it. My life felt as blurry as my tear-soaked contacts, but the one thing that was clear was that I was keeping this baby.

I was worried how Bryan would handle the decision I'd made; it did affect him too. I wasn't sure if he would be mad, but maybe I could find a way to show him that this wasn't necessarily a bad thing. We could be a family. We could be the parents that neither of us had. Maybe it was just the motivation he needed to become that good person I knew was trapped inside him. Maybe he would put his life of crime and drugs behind him and focus on the new life we'd created together.

I was so naive.

That was one of the bigger fights we'd had thus far. Words were yelled as things were thrown about the room. As timing would have it, a thunderstorm was passing through. A clap of thunder and a slamming door sent everything in the room shaking. I sat cross-legged on the curb just outside our motel room, trying to control my crying. I watched as the dark clouds disappeared, revealing the blue sky it was hiding. The crying turned into silent tears and sniffles. I'd begged for a sign from God that I was making the right decision, and I guess I got one.

I grabbed my knees and began to sit up when I saw a little bird about three feet away from me. It sat motionless on the pavement, eyes darting around, feathers ruffled. It looked just as scared as I was. I walked slowly over to it, its stillness puzzling me. I thought maybe it had been stunned by the loud clap of thunder that signaled the end of the storm. I bent down, reaching my hand out to offer comfort. Still, it didn't budge. I scooped my fingers underneath its soft belly and picked it up, cupping it in my hands. I sat back down on the curb, tenderly stroking its tiny head with the tip of my finger.

Was I crazy?

Or was the bird actually enjoying this?

My tears had dried, and my sniffles subsided. I sat there, petting this bird. I knew this was a sign, but I couldn't figure out what it meant. I heard the door open behind me, signaling fear throughout my body. Bryan stepped out looking to continue our fight and then stopped abruptly once he saw me. His demeanor changed as he laid eyes on me cradling the bird.

"Where'd you get that?"

"I didn't *get* it. It just came to me."

He sat down next to me, sharing this moment of wonder. He reached over to pet the bird as well, smiling in disbelief. The bird sensed it was ready to take flight shortly after. It jumped out of the safety of my hands and fluttered off, leaving us in silence.

"I'm sorry," he said softly.

"Yeah, me too."

With those words, the decision was final.

Chapter 9

We were in the final days of our job in South Bend. The store was sparse, sprinkled with random pieces of furniture and unwanted decor. Up front by the cashier station was the only full room with mismatched chairs, a sofa, and a working TV that the sales people would sit around and watch when the showroom was slow. We'd just opened the doors to the store and the sales people congregated nearby, drawing straws to see who was to get the first customer who walked in.

I walked over and turned the TV on, setting the remote on the coffee table in the center of the display. The sound of the news report echoed through the store, and though the details were unclear, it was evident that something was wrong. I looked over at the sales team, who had begun to sprint over in my direction to see the horror that was being televised. I turned around and joined them. We sat there silently staring at the screen. They'd just shown footage of the second plane crashing into New York City's Twin Towers.

As the news unfolded, emotions ran high. The whole world stopped. As they announced that a third plane had hit the Pentagon, the room got heavy. Those of us who were being transferred to Arlington would be minutes from the third crash site. Worry and fear spread through everyone. It was too hard to watch, but we needed to know what was happening. A few sales people had left the room to make phone calls to family members.

I turned and headed back to my cashier station, noticing that the men in the warehouse had come in to watch what was happening. I glanced at Bryan, who didn't seem to be too worried about the situation, and continued on to my seat at the computer. Just then, the phone rang.

It was my mother.

"Holly? Are you okay? Are you pregnant?"

I sat there for a brief moment and finally answered.

"Yes… and yes."

I hung up the phone.

Two weeks later, we were packing up our motel room and loading our car up to head east to Virginia. I was excited about the upcoming road trip, but also nervous as we were unaware of what awaited us. The recent tragedy cast a shadow over the world and here we were, headed straight into the midst of it. We didn't have much to pack, but nonetheless, our car was full. I placed the last bag in the trunk and shut it with some force to make sure it was good and closed. And off we went to begin our eleven-hour journey to the new motel we would call home.

The motel we were staying in was nothing to write home about: a small room with a full-sized bed, bathroom and shower, and a little table in front of the window. The mini fridge was full of groceries we'd grabbed at a nearby 7-Eleven. After we unpacked the car, we decided to head out to see where our new job was located, among various other sites. I grabbed my disposable camera, and we were out the door.

We weren't but two blocks from our motel when we encountered slowed traffic. Cars had pulled over all up and down the side of the highway and curious onlookers stood outside their vehicles, cameras in hand. We slowed as we approached, trying to see what everyone was looking at. We both figured it was just an accident, maybe a presidential motorcade was coming through. Once we got around the bend, we saw what had everyone's attention.

It was the Pentagon.

With a huge hole in it.

We pulled up on the side of the road, stepping out of the car to get a better look. Smoke still billowed out of the gaping hole, and I could even see papers bustling around in what was left of the rooms that had been hit. A large American flag was draped right next to the site of impact, symbolizing the strength of our nation, giving those terrorists the middle finger. I was overcome with a sense of sorrow. It was sad to see, but I wasn't sad—or angry, for that matter. I just felt sorry as I stared deep into that massive hole. This was the world I was going to be bringing a child into.

Great.

We went sightseeing the rest of the day: Arlington National Cemetery, the Lincoln Memorial, the White House… We even drove past the Watergate Hotel. Arlington was a fun city, full of history, and I was excited to see more of it.

But it never really happened.

Most of our time was spent working and as the weeks went on, my belly grew. I wasn't fitting into my regular clothes, so rather than spending money on maternity clothes, I borrowed Bryan's. We were trying to save as much money as we could before the baby arrived. Nobody seemed to have a problem with what I wore, as long as I was presentable. I would work at the cash register, decorating throughout the store as things were being sold and moved out. I would even help in the warehouse, lifting sofas and chairs onto the loading dock, with my big, pregnant belly hanging out of my shirt.

After we clocked out for the day, I would go with Bryan and the other warehouse workers to a nearby restaurant for something to eat while they talked about who knows what over some beers. Given that I was only eighteen—and pregnant— I was deemed the designated driver. I also didn't have any friends out there besides Bryan, and he didn't want to leave me alone in the motel room giving me the chance to make any, so he would have me tag along. I was grateful for the involvement at the time.

Despite Bryan's claims that he could only produce a boy, my ultrasound proved him wrong. We were expecting a little girl. I took everything my OBGYN said to the utmost extreme. I quit smoking and wouldn't even drink caffeine. I found myself in a smoky restaurant on more than one occasion, sitting there with a napkin over my nose and mouth, thinking that it would block any secondhand smoke from harming myself and the baby growing inside me. I just had to hold out until we finished this job. After that, out plan was to drive down the coast to Florida for a mini babymoon and then head back to Indiana, where we would welcome our little girl.

It was around this time that Bryan started to reminisce about the good old days. He talked about his old friends, particularly the ones he would do drugs with. It was hard to tell if he really missed them or if he missed doing drugs with them. After all, to me, they were more like drug buddies than genuine friends. I guess we had different views on what friendship was. I always warned him that they would all end up dead one day if they didn't quit playing with fire. He wouldn't know until years later that I was right.

I should have known that this was a big red flag. Instead, I just took it as him being lonely and missing home. He started hanging out more with the other guys in the warehouse, coming back to our room later and later. His demeanor was changing in a way that I didn't recognize, but I made a mental note of it. I made every effort to accompany him and his "friends" when they would go out so I could keep a close eye on him.

One day after work, the warehouse guys decided to pull an all-nighter to catch up in the stockroom. In order for them to stay up all night, they had the bright idea to blow coke for "energy," as Bryan put it. I found out when one of them had too much to drink after work and ended up spilling the beans. First, he was smoking weed, and now this.

Now, I'm no rocket scientist, but I do know that doing one thing typically opens the door to doing more things. I was upset and felt so powerless. We were going to be starting a family, and the last thing I wanted was to have Bryan be back on drugs. The last thing I wanted to hear was my mom saying, "I told you so." We were leaving town in two weeks and I was counting down the days, hoping they would pass by quickly. In the meantime, I did the best I could to keep him away from his new friends and occupy his time… mostly failing in my attempts.

Chapter 10

The dresser was empty, toiletries packed away, the room free from our belongings. I made one final sweep to make sure that we weren't forgetting anything before turning in our key. I was glad to leave this place. The last couple of weeks were hard, knowing what was going on and knowing there was nothing I could do about it. I'd waited for this day mostly to get Bryan away from the people encouraging his bad habits. We were heading to Florida and then back to the comforts of Indiana, where I was going to give birth to a baby girl. We said our farewells to our fellow coworkers who were housed at the motel with us and hit the road.

I don't remember much about the drive there, except that we had to stop quite a few times so I could use the restroom. It was an uncomfortable ride for me, to say the least. I couldn't recline the seat a whole lot because of how tightly packed the car was. I attempted to find a comfortable position, trying to relieve the pressure from all the extra weight I was carrying. Between songs on the radio, the topic of baby names came up.

"Jessica," Bryan suggested.

"Great. Let's name our baby after your ex-girlfriend."

Every name he suggested reminded me of someone I didn't like or had been mean to me.

"Okay then… Bry-anna…"

I looked over at him. Was he fucking serious right now?

"You've got to be kidding me."

I struggled to think of a name. Literally anything would be better than what he was suggesting.

"What about… Olivia?"

I only knew one Olivia, and she was so sweet. Plus, it wasn't a name you heard very often. He didn't seem opposed to it, and the more I thought about it, the more I liked it.

We stopped overnight at a cheap motel to get some rest and were back on the road early the next day. We arrived in Key West late in the afternoon, where we booked another room for the night.

I was exhausted. Even so, Bryan pulled me along as we walked down Duvall Street to check the area out. The street was lined with twinkling lights, restaurants, and bars. Music and chatter filled the street, and the smell of Banana Boat sunscreen was in the air. It was a lovely place; one I couldn't really enjoy. Bryan wanted to hit the bars, and I couldn't. I was still only eighteen, and I was also big and pregnant. I ended up going back to our hotel, leaving Bryan to have a good time without me. I washed up and lay down on the bed, my feet swollen from all the walking we'd done.

I'd gained a lot of weight, more than a pregnant woman typically should. In my head, when you're pregnant, you could eat whatever you want, so I did. I looked like I'd been stung by a thousand bees. My face was swollen, and so were my hands, my feet, everything. I was dreading the twenty-four-hour drive we had to make over the next couple of days, but at the same time, I couldn't wait to get home.

I was so blinded by my excitement about going home that I failed to see that Bryan wasn't. Part of the reason we'd made the trip to Key West was to delay being back in our hometown. He always did a lot better when he was away from home as far as drugs went. As much as he would try to hide from them, those friends he reminisced about would come out of the woodwork. They always had hard drugs available that they were willing to share, or at least knew where to get some. He didn't want to go back because he knew what would happen.

To anyone else who visited Valparaiso, it would seem like an upper-class town, filled with big houses, nice cars, and beautiful people. But Bryan saw through the facade to what was going on in the background, to the dark, ugly side of the town and what money can buy you. If he knew one thing, it was that money doesn't make you happy. Everyone he knew who had it was miserable. They put on a show for the outside world while secretly numbing their bitter reality. He knew this because he was one of those people.

It was well past midnight when Byran returned to our room. He stumbled in, flicking on the lights and making a ruckus that inevitably woke me up. He knew we had a long drive ahead of us, but that hadn't stopped him from drinking all night. He was agitated, running his fingers through his hair, clasping his hands over his head, pacing back and forth. I sat up in bed squinting, while waiting for my eyes to adjust to the light. I reminded him that we had to leave in just a couple of hours, and that he should get some sleep. This sent him over the edge.

He began knocking stuff over, yelling things that didn't make any sense. I stood up quickly and yelled at him to stop. He turned and glared at me as he reached for his deodorant on the dresser and proceeded to whip it at my head. I was awake enough that I instinctively put my arms up to shield myself. Tears streamed down my face as I cried out, unsure of what was going on or what I should do. He went into a rage, lifting the mattress off the bed and trying to throw it at me, failing miserably. I tried to make my way to the door to get out, dodging whatever was being flung at me. As I reached for the doorknob, I felt something hit my back. Hard. Right below my shoulder blade, in my rib cage. I fell to the floor with a yelp as I realized what had just happened.

I turned around and looked up where Bryan stood, his fist still clenched. A look of fear washed over his face. He looked down at his hand, and then at me, crumpled on the floor, and started crying. We were both stunned at what he'd just done. Not once had he ever laid a hand on me. Never slapped me like he'd admittedly done to a past girlfriend a few times. Heck, he'd never even called me names and rarely yelled at me, for that matter. He turned away from me and walked to the window, where he stared out at the darkness.

I got up, brushed myself off, and wiped the tears from my eyes. As I reached for the doorknob once more, my hand faltered, and I found myself sinking in guilt. I felt responsible for what had just happened. It was my words that triggered this reaction to begin with. It sounds messed up, but I felt bad for him. I knew he didn't mean to do it. If he hadn't been drinking, it would have never happened.

Right?

I could tell he was disappointed in himself for what he'd just done. And what was I going to do? Leave? With no money, no car, and eight months pregnant? Who would want me like this? Even after I had the baby, who would want to be with an eighteen-year-old single mom high school dropout, as Bryan had pointed out in our past couple of arguments? I weighed my options, or lack thereof.

I let go of the doorknob and accepted defeat. I walked over to the mattress, lifting it back onto the bed, in an effort to restore order. I put the sheets back on, and the pillows, erasing the evidence of what had occurred. After I shut the light off, I slipped under the covers and tried my best to pretend like nothing had happened. Bryan stood staring out the window as I silently cried myself back to sleep before finding out if he ever came to bed.

I woke up early that morning, eyes swollen from crying. I pulled the sheets down to get out of bed, feeling the soreness in my back from the blow I'd taken last night. Bryan was already up. If I had to guess, he didn't sleep much, if at all. I got up to shower and got ready to leave. We moved about the room in silence, packing things up once again for our final trip back home. I blamed myself for the events that had taken place. Maybe if I hadn't told him to go to bed when he got in like I was his mother, he wouldn't have reacted that way. I should have just pretended to be asleep and the whole thing could have been avoided. Had I known how he felt about going back home, then I would have understood the outburst he had and would have handled it better.

Unfortunately, I'm not a mind reader.

Chapter 11

We were back home in Indiana, staying at Bryan's mom's house for a few days until our apartment was ready. Our new place was very outdated. It had that really ugly rust-colored plush carpet that belonged in the 1970s. My grandmother gave us some furniture that was stored in her basement, so we had a couch to sit on and a table to eat at. Given the age of the furniture, it complemented the place well. Very retro.

Once we were all moved in, Bryan started a job doing manual labor for some company he found in the Want ads. We had one car and one cell phone that we shared. Bryan would usually take both to work but would occasionally leave me the phone if I needed to call for a ride to go somewhere.

I spent most of my time getting Olivia's room ready. By this time, I'd reconciled with my mom. She'd come to terms that she was going to be a grandma and began to prepare her house for when her granddaughter would be over. Mom threw a small baby shower for me, so we had all we needed for when baby Olivia was to arrive. The crib was made up with new sheets; onesies and dresses hung in the closet. There wasn't much else I could do. Out of boredom, I would rearrange the room, sometimes on a daily basis.

It didn't take long for Bryan to reconnect with his old friends. He hung out mostly with one of them, Shawn. Shawn was a tall, lanky blond who resembled the monster Frankenstein. He was always nice to me, but he made me feel uncomfortable. I knew what he was up to. I knew his intentions—and they weren't good.

One thing you need to know about people who use drugs is that they never want to use drugs alone. They don't want to be the only one addicted to the poison that took over their lives. If they had a friend doing it with them, they felt less like a piece-of-shit drug addict.

It took me a long time to accept the red flags that were presenting themselves, hinting to me that Bryan was using again. My intuition could sense the change in him when he was on something, regardless of what it was. It was as if I had a sixth sense for it, but I couldn't rely on just my gut feeling. I needed solid proof before I could come forward and confront him. And deep down, I did all I could to keep myself from finding it. If I couldn't find evidence of anything to prove I was right, then that meant I was wrong. I wanted so badly to be wrong for the sake of my daughter and our family. But there are some things you can't ignore no matter how hard you try.

It was just a few days away from my due date. I wanted to run some errands so things weren't so stressful once I got home from the hospital. I wanted to be as prepared as possible, knowing that most of my time would be consumed by caring for a newborn. Bryan stayed home and played video games while I went out.

I pulled into our parking spot and got out to unload the

bags from the trunk. As I reached for the last bag, I noticed something shiny roll underneath some miscellaneous items we stored back there. I set the bags down and sifted under the items until I felt it. I pulled out what appeared to be a silver pipe, about six inches long, narrow, with steel wool stuffed into one end. The end that housed the steel wool was charred and blackened. I touched this part, and as I lifted my finger, I could see that the black had transferred onto my skin. I rolled it between my fingers, studying it. I even smelled it. What in the hell was this? At the time, I had no idea I was playing around with a homemade crack pipe. If I'd known that, I would have marched right up the stairs and lost my shit.

"Here's my God-damned motherfucking evidence!"

Instead, I threw it back in the trunk, slamming it shut. I convinced myself it was just some miscellaneous object left behind from the previous owner. Ignoring any doubts I had, I grabbed all the bags and made my way up the stairs to our apartment without a second thought about it.

Chapter 12

I'd been having contractions going on for two days now. Every time they hit, my back felt like I was being run over by a semi-truck with nails sticking out of the tires. I felt miserable from the lack of sleep. I asked Byran if he would leave the cell phone so I could call my doctor when his office opened. He allowed it and handed me the phone on his way out while I tried to get comfortable on the couch.

I was getting increasingly uncomfortable. I flipped from side to side, sitting up, lying down, propping my feet up. I was writhing in pain each time a contraction hit, when all of a sudden, I pissed my pants.

Pissed.

My.

Pants.

The baby was moving around so much that she'd ended up kicking my bladder and I pissed myself because of it. That's what I thought, anyway. I waddled to the bathroom to clean myself up.

Oh, wait...YOWWWWWWW!

I didn't piss myself...

MY WATER BROKE!

Holy shit!

What was I going to do? I had no car. I had no way to get to the hospital!

Wait… The cell phone!

I waddled back to the living room, grabbed the phone, and frantically began dialing the only number I knew to call: my mom's. She had taken a job as a visiting nurse and answered just as she pulled into the driveway of one of her patients. Through labored breathing, I frantically informed her that my water had broken, and that Bryan had gone to work. I'm pretty sure I heard her wheels squeal as she peeled out of her patient's drive en route to my apartment. She made it there in record time too. She helped me into the car and took off toward the hospital. Every time I had a contraction, she slowed the car down, coaching me on how to breathe.

What was she doing?

JUST FUCKING DRIVE!

I'd called Bryan's boss and given him the news that I was going into labor. He went to relay the message himself. I was already in the hospital room waiting as the nurses paged my doctor. More contractions. I was in agony. I squeezed my mom's hand so hard I felt her bones crack. I begged the nurse to give me something, anything, knock me out, I didn't care. The pain was unbearable. They'd paged my doctor six times before he finally showed up.

"Hey, Holly, what are you doing here?"

"Oh, you know, just having a baby…*Where in the hell have you been?*"

The nurse told the doctor they'd paged him a few times. He pulled out his pager and hit a few buttons on it.

"Well, wouldn't you know it, the batteries are dead," he said lightly and laughed.

Really?

This is no laughing matter! There is an alien in my belly trying to claw its way out of me!

My stomach visibly rolled as she flipped around, searching for her way out.

After my doctor assessed my condition, he delivered the news that my window of opportunity to get an epidural had passed. This baby was coming out whether I was ready or not. I had to endure the remainder of childbirth without the relief I'd hoped for. Amid the flurry of activity, Bryan had finally appeared at the door. My mom stayed next to me as the nurses came to my aid.

PUSH! PUSH!

So, I did. With each push my muscles strained, my face burning from holding my breath, panting in between rounds. Again. And again, trying not to push unless I was instructed to. At one point, I even had to get up and straddle a chair for a bit because the doctor didn't like the way Olivia was situated. The nurses helped me back onto the bed once he thought she was in a better position.

PUSH! PUSH!

I was tired. I didn't have the strength to keep going, but I had no choice. My mom and the nurses continued to encourage me as my body went limp from exhaustion.

And then?

Oh, no, am I...

I am...

I think I'm gonna shit all over this bed. I gotta suck her back in!

PUSH! PUSH!

"I can't!"

"Yes, you can. Come on. One… two… three…"

"No, you don't understand… I feel like… like… I'm gonna *poop*! I'm gonna shit all over everyone!"

I said this with a serious sense of urgency and desperation. I didn't care that my vagina was out for everyone and their mom to see. Oh, no. All of these people were about to witness me defecate on this bed. I would never be able to show my face in this town for the rest of my life.

The nurses and the doctor laughed, assuring me that this sensation was normal. Even so, I'd been pushing for nearly five hours. My reserves were drained. I couldn't find the energy to keep going. The nurses were instructed to step in and physically push my belly. And then, a sense of relief.

They laid the baby on my belly and began cleaning her off as the doctor finished whatever he had to do down there. After five long hours, I was handed this chubby little baby. Her eyes squinted under a dark head of hair and her lips quivered as the sounds of new life filled the room. She was more than beautiful. She was a miracle.

Through all of the commotion, I hadn't noticed that Bryan had passed out. A few of the nurses had gone over to tend to him, fanning him with their hands. After he got the color back in his face, he was able to sit up and hold our baby. I'd never seen him so happy. Another nurse came over and took baby Olivia to get her bathed and bundled. My mom had gone out in the waiting area to call our family members and tell them the good news. I lay there, a sweaty mess. I looked over to see Bryan grabbing his keys.

"Where are you going?"

"I'm gonna go ride motorcycles."

And he disappeared out the door.

Chapter 13

We were home: Mom, Dad, and baby. Neither of us realized what parenthood entailed. I spent many long, sleepless nights tending to our crying baby. Diaper blowouts and shirts stained with spit up seemed to be a daily occurrence. Bryan was back at work, and I stayed home to take care of Olivia.

One of the only perks of having a child at a young age was that all of the weight I'd gained was effortlessly melting off me. None of my clothes fit, and I'd resorted to wearing Bryan's clothes once again.

I put Olivia down for a nap while Bryan lay on the couch watching TV. I asked him if he would keep an eye on her so I could run to a nearby department store to buy some new clothes. He pulled the car keys from his pocket and tossed them in my direction. I promised I would only be gone for an hour at most. I could trust him with her for an hour, right?

WRONG.

Remember that sixth sense I told you about?

I got in the car and made my way down the road. I was so happy to finally be getting something new to wear, but I couldn't swallow this bad feeling I had. Its sharp edges stuck in my throat. Something didn't feel right deep down in my soul and I couldn't explain it. I got halfway to my destination before I decided to turn around and head back. I had to get home fast. I didn't know why, but I knew it wasn't good.

I could hear the faint sounds of Olivia crying as I pulled up to the apartment.

I rushed upstairs and swung the door open. Byan was passed out on the couch, and Olivia was crying her little head off in her crib in the other room. I'd been gone a total of fifteen minutes. Fifteen minutes. I couldn't even trust him with her for fifteen minutes. I grabbed Olivia out of her crib to calm her crying. I packed up her diaper bag and loaded her in her car seat, deciding to take her with me. On the way out, I walked over to where Bryan lay sleeping and shook him awake.

He woke up dazed, eyes glossed over. I knew he'd done something. Smoked something. Taken something. Some sort of pill, maybe. How was I supposed to take care of a newborn *and* a grown ass man, not to mention myself? Here it was, another giant red flag waving right in front of my face.

I dismissed it, changing my focus to the things I could control. I looked over at Olivia, cooing in her car seat. She was my reason to hold onto hope. I had to find a way to push through whatever challenges lay ahead. For her.

I did my best to keep our little apartment a safe place. We'd been there for a little over two weeks now. I told Bryan I didn't want Shawn coming over anymore, forcing him to leave to go hang out with him elsewhere. Olivia was asleep in her crib while I was in the kitchen making a quick bite to eat while I had the chance. Bryan walked through the door, just getting home from hanging out with Shawn, and I prepared a plate for him as he made his way over to join me at the table.

Bryan was moving in slow motion. As he raised the fork to his mouth, he was on the verge of falling asleep mid bite. A quick moment of awareness would hit him, and he would snap out of it briefly, but he would then fall right back into his odd behavior. I didn't know what was wrong with him, but there was that feeling again. It was about 7:00, and I told him to go to bed to sleep off whatever was wrong with him. He got up and made his way down the hallway and into the bathroom, locking the door behind him.

What happened next would change our lives forever.

Chapter 14

I did the dishes and tidied up the kitchen. Bryan had been in the bathroom for about thirty minutes. I remained unconcerned as I continued to check on Olivia while I got myself dressed for bed. An hour passed, and Bryan remained in the bathroom. I walked up to the door and pressed my ear against it, slowing my breathing in an attempt to hear what was transpiring on the other side.

Silence.

I started knocking on the door while calling out his name. "Bryan? Bryan…are you okay?"

No answer.

Did he fall asleep on the toilet?

I'd heard of people doing this but never witnessed it myself. He was falling asleep at the table during dinner, so I convinced myself he'd done just that. I walked away and went into our bedroom to get ready for bed.

I awoke to the sound of thumping coming from the other side of the wall that the bedroom shared with the bathroom. It was early morning, and I lay there wondering what it could be as the noise subsided.

Old pipes?

I figured Bryan woke up and went to sleep on the couch to avoid waking me up when he returned to bed. I pulled the sheets off me, getting up to check on him and Olivia. The door was still closed as I began to pass the bathroom. Curious, I reached my hand out and turned the handle. It was still locked.

He couldn't still be in there, could he?

I hurried to the living room hoping to see him covered with a blanket on the couch, but the couch was empty. I ran back to the bathroom and began to beat on the door, my voice rising, and I called out his name.

"Bryan? *Bryan, open the door!*"

Silence.

Then the thumping sound resumed.

Something was terribly wrong.

The door wouldn't budge. I tried everything. I tried swiping a credit card between the strike plate and the latch, but it didn't work. I managed to find a bobby pin and attempted to pick the lock. That didn't work either. I was out of options, so I went to my last resort. I ran to our bedroom closet and grabbed a hammer. I started hurling it at the door, as quietly as I could, trying not to wake up the baby. I failed. I could hear her soft whimpers through the hallway. I left my post to get a bottle ready for her. I skillfully propped her up on some pillows, placing the bottle in her mouth so I didn't have to hold it, making sure she seemed comfortable before I resumed the task at hand. I ran back to the bathroom door, where the hammer lay waiting on the floor. Just before I was about to deliver another forceful blow, the handle started to turn.

"*Bryan! Are you okay?*"

I dropped the hammer, narrowly missing my toes, grabbed the doorknob, and pushed the door open. Something was blocking my path, preventing me from entering. I pushed harder, determined to break through the resistance until I could finally squeeze through.

There, lifeless on the floor, lay a red flag that I couldn't ignore.

Chapter 15

I'd never seen a dead body before, but I assumed this was what it looked like. Bryan lay curled up in the fetal position. His face was a dull gray, and his oily skin glistened in the bathroom light. His hair stuck to his forehead, wet with sweat. His eyes, barely visible, were bloodshot, rolling in the back of his head as he drifted in and out of consciousness. His lips were a dark shade of blue, dry and cracked, with white, foam-like saliva crusted in the corners of his mouth. Whatever life he had left in him was clinging on by a thread.

A tourniquet and three insulin needles were strewn about on the floor near the base of the toilet. A lighter lay on the sink next to the cell phone and a spoon that was charred black on the underside from preparing the heroin. Bryan had passed out and fallen off the toilet after shooting up more than he could handle. The chemical substance had triggered a series of epileptic-like seizures, causing his body to thrash against the wall, creating the thumping sound I kept hearing. As he faded in and out of consciousness, he'd somehow managed to find the strength to crawl to the door and open it before being swallowed by the darkness again. I looked around at the scene in front of me, finally facing what I'd been making excuses for.

He hadn't talked much about his history with drugs. And when he did, you would have thought he was talking about a fond memory he held dear to his heart. The warm, peaceful feeling. The weightlessness. All his worries washed away with a single injection. Every time he used, he'd been trying to reach the high he had the first time his friend Tyler had shot him up. He was chasing the dragon. But this time, he'd found himself in a losing battle with that dragon. He was knocking on death's door, and I had to act quickly.

I grabbed the cell phone off the sink and dialed his brother.

No answer.

I called again.

"Come on, Justin!"

Voicemail.

I called his brother's roommate who, of all people, was Tyler.

Yes. That Tyler.

The guy who introduced Bryan to drugs in the first place. Tyler had cleaned his act up a while back and was making an effort to do something with his life. He answered on the second ring.

"Yo, Bryan, what's up?"

"I need Justin, *now!*" I shouted, holding back tears.

Hearing the panic in my voice, he asked me what was wrong. I told him. He and Justin had told me previously that if anything like this ever happened, to call them first.

Not the cops.

Not 911.

He hung up and in a matter of minutes, he and Justin were at the door. They rushed into the bathroom, picking Bryan up off the bathroom floor and laying him on the couch. Justin attempted to get Bryan to snap out of it, slapping his face and yelling at him to wake up. Despite Tyler's own sobriety, he still maintained the mentality of a drug addict. He went into the bathroom and grabbed the tourniquet and needles, taking them out onto the balcony, where he tossed them up onto the roof. In the event the police showed up, they wouldn't be able to charge Bryan with possession of hypodermic needles and drug paraphernalia.

By this time, Bryan began showing signs of life. He stirred slightly before projectile vomiting and foaming at the mouth like a rabid raccoon. Tyler rushed over to help, while a stressed but calm Justin got up and approached me. He grabbed me by the shoulders and looked me square in the eye.

"Pack your and Olivia's things and get out of here. I want you to stay away from him; he's no good for you."

And I did just that.

I hastily threw some of my things in a bag and stuffed Olivia's diaper bag with diapers and wipes. As I went to grab her out of her crib, I looked out the window, asking myself if things could get any worse. As luck would have it, they did.

Pulling up to our apartment was my mom, just stopping by just to check in on me and the baby.

Perfect fucking timing.

There was no way to hide this situation or explain it away.

Fuck my life.

I tried to intercept her at the door, but Justin and Tyler were already trying to get Bryan down the stairs and into the car to transport him to the hospital. My mom took one look at Bryan and immediately knew what had happened. Justin told my mom that he would handle everything as this wasn't the first time this had happened. My mom helped me put my things into her car before driving me back to her house.

Mom probed me for answers during the whole ten-minute drive, but I sat there silent, emotionless. I spent that short car ride recounting all of those red flags I'd ignored.

The hanging out with his old friends.

The strange behavior.

The pipe in the trunk.

The incident when I tried to go shopping.

Now this.

He'd forced me to take action against him. I didn't want to expose my child to this kind of environment. I couldn't risk the chance of her discovering her father half dead on the bathroom floor. I didn't want her first heartbreak to be at the hands of her own father. Most of all, I didn't want her to follow in his footsteps.

It was over.

It had to be.

And as much as I loved him, I hated him for being so God-damned selfish.

Bryan remained hospitalized for two weeks as the doctors tried to reverse his organ failure. He had the internal organs of a seventy-year-old man at the age of twenty-two. His kidneys had shut down, forcing him to be on dialysis twice a day. Once he was coherent, the doctors delivered the grim news about his condition.

He developed a condition called compartment syndrome on one side of his body that would require surgery. The doctors explained that this happens when you lie on one side of your body for an extended period of time and all the blood and fluid in your body settles on that one side. This causes that side of the body to swell. In other words, his leg had swelled so bad that they had to cut it open to relieve the pressure before the skin ripped open by itself. They planned to harvest skin near his groin to graft over the incision.

He okayed the surgery and signed the waivers, and they began to prepare him for the operating room. As they wheeled his bed down the hallway and into the brightly lit OR, they injected the first step of the anesthesia into his IV. That's when he heard something he probably shouldn't have. The surgeon had entered the room just as he fell into a deep, controlled sleep.

"If he doesn't care about his own life, why should I?"

He had a good point.

Chapter 16

I was back at my mom's house. As mad as I was at Bryan, I still loved him. Staying away from him was hard. I knew he wasn't this terrible person; I could see it in him even if he couldn't. He was so smart; brilliant even. I just needed to find a way to get him to apply himself in other ways, redirecting him away from criminal mischief and drugs. I decided to give him one more chance to clean up his act and be a part of the family we'd created.

I went to the hospital a few times to visit, but it was difficult packing Olivia up and hauling her there. Even when I did go, I couldn't stay very long. There were always people there to visit him when I arrived: family, friends, ex-girlfriends of his. I couldn't control who could come to visit him. His drug buddy, Shawn, even showed up once, and both Justin and I let him know how unwelcome he was and how we felt about him with one look.

Another unexpected visitor was my old friend who had introduced Bryan and me, Natalie. I hadn't seen or talked to her in quite a while. Bryan didn't want me to hang out with her because to him she was a whore. He didn't want her bad habits rubbing off on me. She and I would sit and chat while we waited our turn to be called into his room, since he was limited as to the number of people he could have in there. Even though I was the mother of his child, I still had to wait my turn.

The surgery was successful, avoiding any complications. After a few more days in the hospital, his health was on the mend. There was no more need for dialysis as his kidneys started to work again, and he was gaining strength in his leg with the physical therapy sessions. Once he was able to walk on his own, he was discharged and moved back in with his mom, where the visitors started to trickle down. I gave him the keys to our car so he could get to his follow-up visits without a problem. I had the baby, but I was able to find rides when I needed them. I would leave Olivia with my mom or sisters in order to go over there to take care of him. I would have brought her with me, but they smoked in the house. I didn't want her little baby lungs inhaling all the secondhand smoke that I'd so desperately tried to shield her from during my pregnancy. Some of the people who came by were people I didn't even want to be around, so I felt it best to leave her behind, where it was safe.

Out of all of those people, I began to notice that Natalie would always seem to be there. I thought nothing of it. Given her history with Justin, it was clear she was still hung up on him pretty bad. So, I just assumed that this was her way of trying to weasel her way back into his life. Even though Bryan thought she was a whore, they were still friends.

I went over there one day, leaving Olivia behind with my sisters so I could have a break. Bryan's health was almost back to normal besides a slight limp. He wasn't able to pick me up, so I walked the three miles to his mom's house. Natalie was already there when I arrived. The three of us sat down in the downstairs living room. Bryan and I were on the couch and Natalie was in a chair behind me, discussing our weekend plans, the challenges of being back at home, and our future aspirations.

I watched Bryan as he spoke, taking notice of his shifty eye contact. I could see his shoulders tense up as his eyes darted between Natalie and me. He abruptly stopped mid-sentence, slumping his shoulders and bowing his head, burying his face in his hands. He looked up at me with remorse in his eyes. I just sat there, unsure of what was about to unveil in front of me. Bryan stood up, breathing heavily, rubbing the nape of his neck before he finally spoke the truth. He confessed that he'd succumbed to Natalie's whorish ways and slept with her behind my back during one of her many visits.

There it was.

It was as if all of those red flags were shot like an arrow through my heart.

Ouch.

Talk about a punch to the gut.

But this was more than that. It felt like someone cut my abdomen open and all my insides were falling out.

Right there. On the floor.

Heart and all.

I sat there stunned, my body buzzing from what I'd just heard. Was this some kind of sick joke? No one was laughing, though. I peered at him, trying to distinguish if he was genuinely sorry like he was saying. Then I turned and looked at her. Right through to her White Trash, swampy ass, home-wrecking heart. I'd hoped my glare would burn a hole through her, catching her on fire, causing her to choke on her own ashes.

Instead, she stayed seated, looking right back at me with her beady, rat-like eyes, like she'd done nothing wrong.

You fucking bitch!

What pushed Bryan over the edge was Natalie, my supposed friend, sitting behind me and making lewd gestures at him while I wasn't looking. Bryan might not have always had the best judgment on certain things, but his judgment on certain people was spot on. He and I had argued more than once about her. I would defend my friend from his accusations of ill intentions and promiscuity, only to add her to the list of people I wasn't allowed to hang out with. Now he was hanging around her, and lo and behold, he went and proved himself right without effort.

I thought she was my friend. I thought he loved me.

Well, I guess I thought wrong.

I sat there soaked in humiliation.

I didn't really know what to do next. The situation had taken an awkward turn. I thought I would be mad, or at least more upset than I was. I still wanted to believe this was a twisted joke, but seeing Bryan so upset told me it wasn't. What I wanted to do was punch her in her acne-riddled face. Instead, I stood up and grabbed my purse off the couch, slinging it over my shoulder as I headed toward the door. I stepped outside and took a deep breath, trying to steady my racing thoughts as I shut the door behind me. I half expected Bryan to come after me, begging for my forgiveness, pleading with me to take him back. But he didn't. He knew that there would be no coming back from this. So… guess that was it.

The actual end of whatever future he and I had together.

And with that thought, I started making the trek back home.

Chapter 17

I was able to enroll in an adult education program where I completed the last three classes I needed in order to get my high school diploma. With hard work and persistence, I finished just in time to be able to graduate with my original graduating class. However, I opted out of walking the stage or attending the ceremony in order to save myself from the embarrassment. I was determined to get my life back on track and was lucky enough that I hadn't let it slip too far out of control.

I was fortunate to have support from my mom and sisters while living at home. I was able to get a job and work as many shifts as I could, even having time to get out and live life a bit. Sometimes I would say I had to work when I didn't, still showing up there to hang out with everyone. I would sit at the designated employee table in the bar and drink. I wasn't twenty-one, but no one cared besides one of the uptight managers who was a friend of the owner's. I was trying to put the pieces of my splintered heart back together. It turned out alcohol was the only glue that seemed to hold things together for me. I found myself self-medicating more frequently, trying to forget what I'd gone through by numbing away any emotions I had left toward Bryan.

Bryan continued to call me throughout the week, even after he and Natalie became official and she'd moved into his mom's basement with him. He had hopes of changing my mind, testing the waters to see if I wanted to get back together with him. During one of his calls, I flat out asked him why he insisted on calling me for small talk. I was trying to move on with my life, yet there he was, like a stubborn stain you couldn't wash off your shirt. Besides, didn't he have Natalie to talk to now? I supposed her conversation wasn't nearly as good as mine. He yelled back at me, saying something he would soon regret.

"But I don't want her. I want *you*!"

As he was saying this to me, Natalie walked into the room where he was hiding on the phone.

"Shittttt…." Bryan uttered.

All I heard after that was her yelling obscenities at him. "Fuck you, you fucking asshole!"

She yelled at him while trying to wrestle the phone out of his hands.

I sat there on the other end laughing, before hitting the button to end the call.

The phone calls after that weren't the same. He was angry, as if I was the one responsible for ruining the life he could have had. He resented me for the life he was now stuck with, threatening to come and take Olivia when I least expected it. He called repeatedly, waiting for my mom to answer just so he could call her a cunt, throwing the same threats at her. He was back on drugs and had Natalie hooked on them right along with him, leaving me terrified. We received so many threatening phone calls that we ended up having to file police reports just to keep a record of them in case anything ever did happen.

It wasn't long after this that I found out Bryan and Natalie had gotten married.

Was I surprised?

Nope.

There is no better way to fix a shitty relationship than to make it officially official. Two drug addicts, uniting as one. Natalie had finally found a way to get into that family. She accepted that Justin wanted nothing to do with her anymore, so she went for the next best thing: his brother. In her sick, twisted mind, marrying Bryan allowed her to still be close to Justin. How fucked up is that?

Her family was a whole different kind of train wreck. Her mom and three sisters were all pill-popping alcoholics, just like her. She was a product of her environment and didn't stand a chance. She wasn't always a horrible person, though. We had many laughs together, many fun times. But when it came to holding any accountability or responsibility, that's where we differed. I was also far less willing to experiment with anything, unlike her. Just like with Bryan, I was guilty by association.

Drama followed her and her family like a vulture circling its prey. They were no strangers to law enforcement, engaging in verbal and physical altercations with each other and calling the cops on each other. One of them even put roadkill on the other's front porch. They stopped on the side of the road to scoop up a decayed racoon carcass and then put it on their front porch. I mean, they really held no boundaries when it came to how low they would go to try and ruin each other's day. I'd witnessed it firsthand when she and I were friends.

I actually felt kind of bad for him knowing that this was the family he was stuck with. Even though I hated that they were married, I made an honest effort to be his friend, for Olivia's sake. When I saw that their relationship only fed their need for drugs and chaos, I decided it was best to keep myself and Olivia as far away from them as possible. I filed for full custody, sending Bryan into a drug-fueled rage.

Mom and I were still butting heads, but we could at least agree that we needed to keep Olivia safe. It was during this period when my mom presented me with a plan. She'd talked with an attorney about the whole situation. They suggested that my mom take temporary custody of Olivia. By doing so, it would prevent Bryan's ability to show up at any given time to take her as he was threatening to do. She even had the necessary papers drawn up, leaving me with the simple task of signing them.

It made sense.

And I didn't want to do it.

So, I didn't.

I didn't want to do it mainly because I didn't want my mom to have that much control over anything or anyone in my life. I knew that if I signed those papers, she would find a way to hold it over my head, using it as leverage in one way or another. I know what you're thinking: "But it's your mom. Would she really do something like that?"

Yes. Yes, she would.

Bryan's threats to show up and take Olivia didn't stop. By this time, she was four years old, and I was still constantly worried anytime I was away from her. My file of court documents had ballooned to the point that it was overflowing and the file folder was ripping. It contained motions requesting full custody, continuances, child support revisions, and so on. All of this paperwork and money spent with little to show for it.

I had to work and couldn't necessarily take Olivia with me all the time. She would join me at work on occasion when I didn't have a sitter, helping me around the restaurant by placing silverware in the basket and watching TV in the back booth that we kept open for staff to sit and take a break. She was my little helper, and everyone loved having her around.

She was in kindergarten now, attending the same elementary school that my sisters and I had gone to. It took her no time to become one of her teacher's favorite students. I would pick her up after school and listen to her teachers' praises of how well-mannered and helpful she was in class. I was just happy that none of what was going on with her dad and me had affected her negatively.

The street was lined with cars waiting for the sound of the bell signaling the end of the school day. Parents waited on the playground to walk home with their kids. I stood on the sidewalk by myself. I was the youngest parent there, and besides my daughter being a student at the same school as their kids, I had nothing in common with the other parents. I would look around at them and couldn't help but be a little jealous of the happy families they seemed to be. I would stand off to the side, watching the cars drive by, and my attention would go to the door where the kids would come piling out looking for their parents. Just before the bell rang on this day, I recognized a face in a car that drove by and my stomach sank.

It was Bryan.

I rushed up to the school door, pushing myself past the kids eagerly trying to exit. I made my way to Olivia's teacher, who was standing at the door bidding farewell to all of her students.

She could tell by the look on my face that there was a problem. I briefly told her the situation just as Bryan was walking up. He demanded that Olivia be handed over to him. I did the best I could to keep the situation from getting out of hand, begging him to meet me at my mom's house, where we could discuss things.

He wouldn't.

I pleaded with him to go to my car and not make a scene in front of Olivia's classmates.

He refused.

Despite my pleas, he made a scene. He yelled at me, yelled for Olivia to come out to him. She was still inside packing up her backpack, oblivious to the commotion outside. Sensing the tension, the other parents retrieved their children and hurried off before things escalated.

Olivia's teacher handled the situation with remarkable composure. I could tell this wasn't the first time something like this had happened on her watch. In her soft, calming voice, she told Bryan that Olivia would stay in the classroom until she felt it was safe for her to be released. In the meantime, the police were on their way. Relief washed over me as she spoke. I knew it wasn't over, but I was so thankful for the way her teacher handled the situation.

Upon hearing what the teacher had to say, Byran stormed back to his car and took off. I followed the teacher inside the school and into the classroom, where Olivia was playing with other kids who were part of the after school program. I took a moment to explain the situation to the teacher. She suggested that I make an appointment to talk with the principal so we could discuss ways to handle this if it were to happen again. The next day, I found myself in the principal's office doing just that.

I felt like I had no other option than to take my mom up on her offer.

I had to sign those papers.

You know, the ones Mom had her attorney draw up. What if I hadn't been there to intercept Bryan at the school? He could have taken Olivia and disappeared, and no one could do anything about it. By signing those papers, I wouldn't have to worry about that happening. I played out every scenario of what could possibly happen if I didn't sign them, and each one gave me a stronger reason as to why it was the best thing to do. I talked with my mom and made sure that custody could be given back to me at any time; that this was, in fact, a temporary measure. She assured me it was, and with that, I placed all my trust in a piece of paper.

It was only a few days after signing and filing those documents that she kicked me out.

Me. Not Olivia.

Since she had temporary custody, I was forced to leave my daughter behind. It broke my heart. I stayed with a few friends for a bit, so I could stay close and visit her when I could. My mom would occasionally let me take her with me, letting me stay over some nights with her.

I understand now why she did it, but at the moment, I hated her. I felt betrayed, tricked into signing without full disclosure of what she intended to do. But she was right to do so. I needed to get my shit together. My decision-making skills lacked calculation and estimation. My ambition to put myself in a better situation was clouded by a lifestyle of partying. But most of all, I wasn't mature enough to be a parent. I was a kid trying to raise a kid. It was time to grow the fuck up.

Chapter 18

I'd reached out and reconciled with my dad, and after agreeing to a long list of my stepmom's rules, I moved back into their house. My dad even offered to help me sign up for some courses at the community college, and if I kept my grades up, he would pay for it. I felt like I had some real support for once. I started classes in criminal justice a few nights a week and held up my end of the bargain.

I was still working my job as a hostess at a local sports bar. I didn't make much, but it was enough to get by. It was a fun place to work, and I'm still friends with my old coworkers from there to this day. Some of my best friends came out of that shit hole. We were all battling similar demons, and instead of facing them alone, we were there to help each other. If you made a stupid decision, it wasn't all that bad because you didn't make it alone. It would become something that you could laugh about at work the following day.

We got drunk together. We got high together.

These were my people.

I didn't feel so alone anymore.

I was at work, seating families at their table when the phone rang. I answered it thinking it would be a to-go order, but instead, it was my dad.

"Holly, you need to come home."

I'd just got to work; I couldn't leave now. I could sense something was wrong by the tone in his voice, so I asked if everything was okay.

"I don't know, but all your stuff is being thrown outside."

This again? What is it with people and throwing my stuff outside? What in the hell did I do now?

I sped home, mentally going through my morning and what could have possibly set my stepmom off. As I pulled up, I could see my dad trying to console and calm her as she angrily tossed bags and articles of clothing out onto the driveway. I parked and got out of the car, standing there wondering why she was so mad. It never dawned on me that the whole time I was back, she'd been searching for an excuse to throw me out, no matter how small. A few seconds later, the police showed up. It wasn't just any officer—it was my teacher.

"Hi, Lieutenant," I muttered.

Once he recognized who I was, he asked me what was going on, and I told him the extent of what I knew. He was able to calm my stepmom down enough to get her to allow me to go inside and pack up the rest of my things. She insisted on supervising me, watching my every move and taking note of every item I packed. My teacher remained by her side to make sure nothing escalated.

I was his star student this semester. I got good grades and was really the only one who participated in class. He started to help me carry some things to my car and that's when my stepmom lost her shit. Wailing and hollering at the top of her lungs, she claimed that everything I was taking was hers. How she was the one who had called the police and they should be helping her, not me. The lieutenant set down the box he'd been carrying and reached in, pulling out one of my more revealing tank tops.

"Ma'am, I highly doubt you'll be wearing this anytime soon."

Try not to laugh, try not to laugh...

I had to turn away just to hide the look on my face.

She did NOT like this. She continued on with her theatrics, taking aim at the both of us. Threats of all sorts spewed out of her. She was escorted to another room while he continued to help me load up my car. I didn't have much, so it didn't take too long. He shut the trunk and looked over at me.

"I take it you won't be in class tonight?"

I let out a heavy sigh. "Probably not."

Chapter 19

I was sent to live with my aunt and uncle for the sole purpose of straightening my life out. Their no-nonsense attitudes would be just what I needed to get my act together. Although my mom saw this as a form of punishment, I liked living with them. They were actually the family mine used to be. Dinner was on the table every night and everyone was there, sitting in their designated seats. They spent time with each other watching a show or playing a game. It was a nice change. To me, they weren't even that strict. Helping my aunt paint their sunroom and holding a job were their only requirements besides being respectful. No big deal. I still went to my serving job almost every day, and painting was something I really enjoyed. On top of that, they were smokers just like me, so I seemed to fit right in.

A few weeks later, it was decided that I would move in with my grandmother. My grandfather had passed away and even though she was getting along just fine alone, we felt it would be best for her to have some company around. I was okay with this. And so was everyone else. If anyone could whip me into shape, it was my grandma.

I shared a strong bond with my grandma. When I was born,

she told my other grandma to "move out of the way, Phyllis, this one's mine," a story my mom often recalls. To me, I was her favorite out of all of my sisters and cousins. Was this true? Probably not. But my name was on her handwritten call list before any of them, so I took it as a sign that I was.

I would get home from work to my grandma halfway through a bottle of wine. I would sit with her, listening to her stories as Elvis Presley sang to us from her record player. She'd smoked cigarettes since childhood but had quit since my grandpa's passing. Occasionally, she would ask me for one of my Camel Lights, and I would always give it to her. She was my grandma. I wasn't about to tell her how to live her life. I did whatever she asked of me.

I didn't go out as much when I lived there. And when I did, I was home at a decent time out of respect. Things were going well for the most part. I was still working as much as possible, seeing Olivia whenever I could.

I ended up staying late at work one night to help power wash the floors with a handful of my other coworkers. We goofed off a bit too much, and I ended up pulling a muscle in my shoulder. I went to urgent care, where they gave me a script for Vicodin and sent me on my way.

I'd never taken this stuff before. It was something I knew people took recreationally, but given what I'd gone through with Bryan, I wasn't about to start taking this for anything other than pain relief. I took it sparingly, only when I couldn't tolerate the pain. I needed it, and it helped.

I'd left my purse on the kitchen table. My grandma went to put it in my bedroom, where she continued to look through it. Maybe she was looking for a cigarette; I don't know. Instead, she found my pill bottle. She didn't have the internet or a computer, so her investigative work consisted of searching through the yellow pages to find the doctor's name. Her research turned up nothing, since he wasn't listed. I was confronted once I woke up from my nap.

"What are these? Where did you get them? I won't tolerate drugs in my house!"

I didn't see the sense in explaining, even though I tried. As much as I loved my grandma, I didn't want to live under her microscope. I didn't want to be the topic of the conversations that were to be had about whether I was addicted to pills or whatnot. I decided to pack my things and figure out what to do next later.

I'd become desensitized, detaching myself from my emotions.

I drove around aimlessly for hours. My music was turned all the way up and the guts of the speakers rattled with the beat. It was the only thing that I seemed to be able to feel. With nowhere to go, I went to the only place where I knew I wouldn't be judged. The one place where I would be welcomed with open arms: the bar.

I had a good thing going for a few days. I would go to work in the morning and offer to work a double shift. That took care of most of my day. When it was time to close up shop, I would go to the bar and stay until closing. To avoid drawing any attention, I parked my car in the farthest spot so no one would suspect there was anyone sleeping in it. I'd hoped they would assume that someone had a little too much to drink and they'd hitched a ride home in order to not catch a DUI. When I needed to shower, I just went to the gym where I was a member and used their facility.

Even though I was getting by, I was tired. I missed my

daughter. And living the way I was wasn't the way to get her back. I knew going back to my dad's house wasn't an option. My friends either still lived at home or didn't have room in their small apartments for me to crash for a while, which left me with no other choice. I would have to go back to the one place on earth I didn't want to be. Even worse, I had to go talk to my mom and beg her to let me come back.

The ultimate walk of shame.

Chapter 20

Despite everything, my job was going well. I'd moved up from hostess to waitress, but that didn't help my drinking problem. My fellow servers and I were hanging out almost every day, having drinks at the bar after work on nights I didn't have to be home by a certain time. Other nights, I would come up with excuses why I got home later than expected, usually saying that I'd ended up having to close for a friend.

My new work friends would introduce me to new groups of people.

And new men.

Stress between my sisters and me was at an all-time high as well. They'd grown tired of my bullshit excuses about why I had to stay late at work and my constant asking them to babysit for me. I didn't see the harm in wanting to go out, especially if Oliva was sleeping. I was young and single, and I needed a break every now and then. But every now and then had turned into almost every night.

Going out was the only way I knew how to meet new people. In that town, there really wasn't any other way to put yourself out there, let alone much else to do. Dating apps weren't a thought yet. And even though I didn't really have the money to spend, I could always find a couple dollars for a beer or two.

Throughout the week, I would frequent the local bars with coworkers and new friends I'd made, hoping to find a connection. Despite always being one of the guys, I still didn't really know how to talk to the opposite sex. So, I did the next best thing—I tried to be funny. And the liquid courage helped. I began paying more attention to my appearance, experimenting with makeup and new hairstyles and dressing more provocatively. Even though I was getting the wrong kind of attention, it didn't stop me from liking it. I was able to use this to suppress any feelings I had left toward Bryan.

I met a few guys, but no one I thought was "the one." We would hang out for a few weeks, our dates revolving around meeting at the bar, until things dissipated and our attention shifted elsewhere. It quickly became apparent that they were only after one thing, preventing any potential for a genuine connection to develop. So, they never led to any kind of real relationship. Things never ended badly with anyone. At the very least, I gained a new drinking buddy.

I found a friend among the crowd of people I hung out with on my nights out. Christy became my companion most nights; she was willing to explore different towns, trying new places and meeting new people. We'd grown tired of the immature men in our town and decided to branch out to see what other areas offered. Whether it was going to the neighboring town or making our way up to Chicago, it added a much needed variety to my life as I continued my search for my missing piece.

Bryan's efforts to disrupt my life were becoming increasingly aggressive. Whatever money I could scrape up went straight to my attorney. The plus side to doing this was that I was able to receive some sort of child support: a whopping $31.00 a month.

It wasn't much, but it was better than nothing. I'd presented Bryan with multiple opportunities to sign over his rights as a father. He wouldn't have to pay child support or live up to any other obligations as long as he just left us alone.

He refused.

So, in and out of court we went.

My attorney and I pushed for supervised visitation. I had doubts about Bryan's claims of being clean and sober, finding it hard to believe that he wasn't using drugs again. Natalie had to take insulin shots multiple times a day to manage her diabetes, giving him access to needles. How could an addict watch someone inject themselves with something, even if it was just insulin, without feeling the temptation to do the same? In my eyes, it was a gateway to relapse. All it would take was a phone call, and he could get his hands on some of that devil's candy.

The other thing I couldn't fathom was Natalie's filthy, disgusting habits. She left needles strewn about on the nightstand, wedged between couch cushions—everywhere. The thought of Olivia being exposed to the potential risk of sticking herself with a used needle was unsettling. I couldn't allow that to happen. Bryan failed to see the validity of my concerns. My actions against him weren't driven by personal motives or financial gain as he accused me of. I was trying to keep my daughter safe.

Chapter 21

I placed my keys in the dish on the table and walked through the metal detector, where another officer used a handheld metal detector to conduct a sweep of my whole body. My attorney was already there, seated outside the courtroom with her briefcase. I grabbed my keys out of the dish and approached her. Once she saw that I was there, she stood up and motioned for me to follow her to a more private area.

"What are the chances that he's using again?" she whispered.

"Very high," I confidently said without hesitation.

She smirked and nodded. Bryan had just arrived, and they were calling both parties to the courtroom.

I'd never been in a courtroom until now. My expectations, shaped by TV shows like *Law & Order*, were of a grand, intimidating chamber with a judge presiding from high up on their podium, holding a gavel, calling for order in the court. Reality was quite different. It was a well-lit room, relatively small, with two long tables centered in the middle of the room. The judge was already seated as we took our seats and the court proceeded like a finely tuned machine.

Bryan had no representation. It was him against me. My

attorney presented facts, detailing his history of misconduct, drug use, and time spent in jail. He sat there, itching to interject, struggling to contain himself. When he was finally given the opportunity to speak, his mental and emotional instability were on full display. His behavior became so disruptive that the judge halted the proceedings until Bryan could compose himself, picking himself off the floor and getting back in his seat.

The judge studied Bryan with a keen eye.

"Mr. Galanis, I am suspending this court session. Given your erratic behavior, I am hereby ordering you to go to the nearest drug testing facility. I am sending orders over now and will give you the address of where you are to go. You are to leave here and go directly there, immediately. No stops. No delays. Go straight there. Court will reconvene once the results of the tests are in. Court is adjourned."

I was flabbergasted.

So was my attorney.

Her plan had been to request a drug test at some point during the hearing, but given Bryan's behavior, she didn't have to. The judge witnessed first-hand the roller coaster of emotions and strange behavior that was on display for all the court to see. Bryan was escorted out of the courtroom by an officer, and the judge had my attorney and me lag behind. He wanted to make sure that Bryan was out of the parking lot before he let us leave, for our own safety.

I went home.

Nothing was accomplished.

What a waste of time and money that I didn't have.

I was back at square one. I spent the rest of my morning worrying about what to do next when my phone rang. It was my attorney with an update. She'd received a call from the court informing her that Bryan had failed to comply with the orders. Yes, he showed up to the drug testing facility... but he was two hours late.

Now, I can't say for certain if he was on drugs that day; I didn't believe he was. Regardless of his poor judgment, I didn't think he would be stupid enough to show up in court high as a kite. After he was given the orders by the judge, he likely did what any person who was about to fail a drug test would do.

He went and bought a one-hour drug detox drink from the local head shop, a well-known method for passing a drug test. These drinks flush your system, making certain drugs undetectable or resulting in an inconclusive test to buy yourself more time. He arrived at the facility with a new haircut. His head wasn't completely bald, but his hair was short enough to reduce the likelihood of them finding traces of anything if they ended up taking a sample. In his efforts to help himself, he couldn't have made himself appear more guilty.

I didn't have to return to court. It was ruled that Bryan was to have supervised visits until further notice. The taste of victory wasn't all I'd hoped it would be. Bryan's supervised visits were few and far between. He was responsible for paying the facility in order to see Olivia. I would get a call from the office notifying me that he paid to schedule a visit, and they were calling to confirm a time. I wouldn't tell Olivia she was going to see him until we were on our way there. I didn't want her to get her hopes up on seeing him. Sometimes we would show up and he would be there; other times he was a no show. My heart broke for her the times he didn't show. At least the staff were nice enough to play with her to make our drive there worth it.

Bryan once asked me what I would tell Olivia when she was older and asked why he and I weren't together. Honestly, I'd never really thought about it. But I didn't have to. I told him that I would tell her the truth: that he was on drugs and chose that lifestyle over being a father and having a family. That I had tried all I could to keep him away from her in order to keep her safe. I wouldn't lie about it, and if she hated me for it, then so be it. I'd never hidden who her father was, and I'd never looked for a "replacement." Anyone I dated knew that Olivia knew who her dad was, and I didn't need them to step in to play the part. I was doing just fine being both mom and dad. I figured I would have time to really think through what I would say and how I would approach it since she was so young. And I did—until I found myself in a situation where I was forced to tell her, whether I was ready to or not.

I'd wished things were different for her. I wanted nothing more than for her to have a stable family and to know both of her parents. I knew that right now, Bryan couldn't be that parent.

As far as I went, I was barely the parent I should have been. Even though my mom remanded custody back to me, I was still partying nearly every weekend, even during the week sometimes, when I should have been home with Olivia. She deserved better from me. Even though I fought so hard to keep her safe, I couldn't seem to find it in myself to step into the role of a loving mother. I'd spent years struggling just to get by; I didn't want her life to be this hard. I knew I couldn't give her the life she deserved. I feared that my efforts to be a mother would only be met with disappointment as she would be subjected to the same hardships that I was dealing with.

Instead of taking any steps to improve my situation, I found myself running, fleeing from my problems. Searching for a way out in the wrong places. Looking for love in the wrong places. I vowed to never put myself in a situation like I'd been with Bryan, ever again.

Never to shoulder the blame for things I didn't do.

Never to let any injustices against me pass unchecked.

It wasn't until a few years later, as I stood reciting my wedding vows, that I came to the painful realization that I'd made the same mistake again.

But this time, it was worse.

Way worse.

Chapter 22

I waited for the bartender to bring me my change. The bar was buzzing with activity, filled with unfamiliar faces and dancing bodies. It was a nice change of scenery from the usual bars my friends and I frequented. The bartender placed my change in front of me as they began to take an order from the next patron. I scooped up my money, pushing a few dollars toward the edge of the bar for the bartender to keep before navigating through the crowd to the table that Christy was saving for us.

We settled into our seats, soaking in the vibrant atmosphere as the music played at a deafening volume, making it nearly impossible to have a conversation. We watched as girls danced, vying for attention from the onlooking guys who had congregated around the dance floor. Christy and I took turns walking around to scope out the place. The dimly lit bar was alive with flashing lights, different colors illuminating the dance floor, while the faint glow of the register and coolers behind the bar offered just enough visibility to discern those nearby.

The DJ had just stepped out from behind his booth, giving us a much needed break from the blaring music. We'd been to this bar once before, but this time, it lacked any of the attractive men we were always on the hunt for.

"I guess that guy over there isn't too bad." I nodded toward two guys sitting at a table across the way.

The one I was referring to seemed slightly drunk, unsteady in his seat. I'd seen the many phases of people under the influence of alcohol given my experience as a bartender. He was older, specks of gray peppered through his black hair, and his laugh revealed a decent set of teeth. Meanwhile, his friend leaned against the table, engaged in their conversation while periodically glancing in our direction.

Christy was the kind of person who could talk to anybody. She was everyone's friend, whether they knew it or not. She had no reservations about approaching someone she didn't know and introducing herself, exactly like she was about to do to these two men. I remained at our table, sipping my drink, until I saw her wave me over to join them.

I'd grown accustomed to being introduced as her "pretty" friend, often followed by a roll of my eyes as I would reach out my hand to offer my name and a handshake. The usual questions followed: Where are you from? What do you do for work? How old are you? It was a quick way of getting to know someone before the music came back on, drowning out any chance of further conversation. Through our exchange, we learned that the guys shared the same first name, were neighbors in the town we were currently in, and were both single.

I sat between Christy and Tom, listening as Tommy recounted a story that he found far more amusing than the rest of us did. Tom and I engaged in flirtatious banter, leaning into each other as we snickered back and forth. The scent of whiskey lingered on his breath, his words blending as he whispered in my ear. The eleven-year age gap didn't turn me off to him. He seemed to have his shit together yet was still immature enough to relate to someone my age.

Our drinks quickly disappeared, prompting another round to be ordered as we continued getting to know each other. The DJ was making his way back to the booth, signaling the impending onslaught of loud music for the crowd to dance to. Tommy kept a sharp eye on his watch before letting Tom know that it was time for them to leave. We exchanged farewells and pleasantries before they made their way toward the exit. Christy and I remained at the table, where we worked on finishing our drinks, when I suddenly felt an arm wrap around my waist.

It was Tom.

Not ready to call it a night, he invited us both to his house to join him for a night cap. Ever the adventurous duo, we chugged the remainder of our drinks and grabbed our belongings, trailing behind Tom as we exited the bar. Tommy had pulled his car up to the entrance to pick Tom up, directing us to follow him once we got into our vehicle.

It was a short trip to his house. Christy drove, keeping close to avoid losing them in the traffic. We wound our way through a subdivision, marveling at the impressive sizes of the homes we passed, until the guiding tail lights turned into a driveway.

His house was a sight to see, boasting grandeur with a veranda enveloping its entirety. We entered through the three-car garage, where a black Buick Grand National was tucked away, later learning it was one of Tom's most prized possessions. Inside, the beauty of the house matched its exterior, featuring granite countertops, rich, dark hardwood floors, and crisp white trim. The decor was minimal yet elegant, with toys scattered in corners serving as evidence that he wasn't the only person who lived there.

I showed myself around as Tom and Christy busied themselves preparing cocktails for us. As I looked around, I came upon a picture of Tom and a young girl, whom I presumed to be his daughter. She appeared to be about the same age as Olivia. I took note of this before making my way back to the kitchen where my drink was waiting for me.

Tommy was sitting on the couch talking with Christy before he excused himself to use the restroom. Tom and I sat on the love seat, swapping stories about our daughters. A few minutes passed, and Tommy hadn't yet returned. Christy volunteered to investigate and walked down the hallway to discover the bathroom was empty.

"He's fine. He went home to his family."

Family? Did we miss something?

With a little persuasion from the alcohol, the truth about Tommy emerged. Despite the nakedness of his ring finger, he was happily married with a baby on the way. His wife was at home next door, awaiting his return so she could rest easy. We wondered if she knew he was out hitting on other women, leaving Christy soured at the lies she'd been led to believe.

It was getting late, and even though Tom's efforts to get me to stay were increasingly convincing, I kindly declined. Before we left, I scribbled my cell phone number on a piece of paper I found on the counter. Christy was already halfway to the car before I finished lacing up my boots. I offered Tom one last hug goodbye.

I stood on the tips of my toes to wrap my arms around his neck. He drew me in close, lifting me up as he embraced me with a tight squeeze. I laughed at his playfulness as he set me back down on the ground. In a fleeting moment, his cheek brushed against mine, and before we knew it, we found ourselves locked in a kiss, his final attempt at getting me to stay. It almost worked.

Almost.

Christy and I spent the car ride home reviewing the events of the night, dissecting Tommy's stories to see if we could have caught his lies earlier and laughing at Tom's sad attempts to woo me into his bed. Even so, I found him charming. He stood out among the crowds of immature and childish men who seemed to orbit my group of friends like piranhas. He portrayed himself as having his life together, bolstered by the cars and house adding to his allure. I continuously checked my cell phone, hoping to see it light up with a text message or incoming call, but it remained silent and dark the rest of the way home.

Chapter 23

It was three days later that I finally received the phone call I'd been waiting for. It was an invitation to dinner with Tom's brother and sister-in-law. Unsure if this was meant to be a date, I decided to treat it as one. Still, I was grateful that there would be other people there to alleviate the pressure of a one-on-one conversation.

I took a shot of vodka to calm my nerves before leaving Olivia with my sister for the evening. I arrived at Tom's house where his brother, Jason, and sister-in-law, Lynn, were scheduled to pick us up. Unsure of where we were going for dinner, I opted to eat something small beforehand in case the menu options didn't suit my taste. It turned out to be a wise decision as the stress of the situation took a toll on my appetite.

Jason and Lynn showed up not long after I arrived. I was surprised to see that Tom and Jason bore no physical resemblance to each other. Jason, short and handsome, took after the Mexican side of their family, while Tom resembled the Italian side. Despite their differences in appearance, they shared the same laugh and sense of humor. Once they were in the presence of one another, it wasn't hard to see that they were brothers.

Lynn, tall and petite, exuded an air of maturity that seemed to compensate for the lack of it among the rest of us. Her dark hair framed her face, and she possessed a motherly presence that proved invaluable, especially when Tom and Jason dove into bouts of immaturity, which I observed sporadically throughout our dinner.

The restaurant was busy, the aroma of garlic filling the air as waiters walked by carrying trays of pasta and fresh-baked bread. Our glasses clinked as we toasted and took a sip of wine before placing them back on the table. I was trying to pace myself; I didn't want to make an ass out of myself on our first date. We placed our orders and made small talk, getting to know everyone around the table little by little. I found myself only reaching for a drink when Lynn did until our dinner arrived, and our attention was diverted to the meal in front of us.

Dinner was good, even though I barely touched it. The wine certainly helped loosen me up, but even so, I couldn't shake off the feeling of being out of place. I was the youngest out of all of us. I made an effort to participate in the conversation, answering questions and asking my own in an attempt to establish common ground. I reassured myself that feeling a bit awkward was normal, considering I'd just met everyone, and convinced myself that our next encounter would be a better one.

The waiter stopped by our table and dropped off our check, signaling an end to our evening. Jason kindly insisted on picking up the tab despite Tom and me offering to pay our share. It was a thoughtful gesture, leading me to think that our meeting had been a success, but I was glad it was over. I was ready to get back to the comforts of my own awkwardness.

We bid our farewells as we got out of the car and headed to the front door. Tom held the door open, allowing me to enter first, and followed me into the foyer. It seemed he wasn't ready to say goodbye just yet, and since I had a bit of time before I had to go home, I accepted his offer to watch a movie.

What movie was it?

I couldn't tell you, since there wasn't a lot of watching going on.

I really tried to behave myself. I didn't want to fuck this up like I'd done so many times before. I had a flawed mindset and thought that being intimate with someone would pave the way to a meaningful relationship. But it was useless. It was a warped way of thinking, and one that never worked out in my favor. The time for me to leave had passed and I decided to stay the night. I would think of an excuse to tell my sister on my way home in the morning.

I brought Olivia with me the next time Tom and I hung out. He had his daughter, and they played together well, giving us plenty of alone time. This became a more frequent occurrence, even when his daughter wasn't there. It was nice that he didn't mind me toting Olivia along and accepted that I was a young mother. He seemed to have a thing for the young ones; his daughter's mother was younger too.

As we continued to hang out with Jason and Lynn, I learned some interesting details about Tom's living situation. It turned out that the house he lived in used to be theirs. Tom moved in after he'd gotten out of jail and was staying there until they sold it.

Yeah, you read that right.

Jail.

I found that out from Lynn, who told me she used to write

him letters and keep in touch with him while he was away. She never gave me any details as to why he was in there, so I went to the source. He explained it away, citing a loophole with the Michigan State laws related to owning a certain type of gun. I had no reason not to believe him. Besides, that was nothing compared to Bryan's rap sheet.

Things were getting serious with Tom. Jason and Lynn sold the house he was living in, prompting him to find a townhouse to rent, conveniently located near my mom's. He approached the topic of us moving in together and I excitedly accepted his offer. It felt like my first real chance at having a relationship with the potential of it evolving into something more, and that was what I wanted more than anything.

Chapter 24

Tom's job as a satellite TV installation technician required him to travel all over to the likes of Illinois, Michigan, and southern Indiana. It wasn't unusual for him to be on the road for several days at a time. I still worked at the sports bar, gradually spending less time with my friends to demonstrate my commitment to my new relationship.

I never thought twice on the nights where he didn't come home. He would simply explain that his job was running behind, and he had to stay in whatever town he was working in for the night. However, my suspicions were aroused when I stumbled upon pictures of various naked women on his computer during one of his nights away. This discovery led me to start questioning the truth behind these frequent overnight stays.

It's easy to look back and wonder what I was thinking, but my investigative skills weren't as sharp back then as they are now, so cut me some slack. After examining the dates on some of the pictures, I discovered that most of them had been taken before we even met, which I couldn't fault him for. The others? Those needed to be explained.

I confronted him about it all when he got home, expecting

a serious discussion. However, he simply laughed it off and dismissed my concerns as insignificant. He reassured me that he loved me and claimed that the pictures were old, with many of them being sent as jokes from his brother and friend. He even offered to delete them immediately if they bothered me so much. True to his word, he promptly deleted the pictures.

As our relationship deepened, so did the intensity of our arguments. The constant back and forth of his love bombing and displays of importance followed by moments of devaluation and belittling had me living in a constant state of anxiety. I began to overthink my every move, which sent me into a spiral of fear and self-doubt. Out of my deep-rooted fear of rejection, I found myself becoming obedient to his demands. The way I looked at it, I did it because I loved him. Sacrificing my own needs to ensure his happiness seemed like a small price to pay. His happiness was more important to me than my own.

It became painfully clear that my happiness meant shit to him. Tom had the tendency to do horrible things and then attempt to blind me with gifts to smooth things over. This pattern became so frequent that my mind struggled to process it all. I found it easier to ignore the ugly truth and focus solely on what I wanted to see, until it got to the point where I could no longer turn a blind eye to the truth.

I knew something was going on with all the late night texts he would receive. He started spending more time in Chicago with his brother, something that I couldn't necessarily complain about since he was family. Hanging out with his brother soon escalated into overnights, when he claimed he stayed at his brother's house. When I would come across hotel receipts I found in his pockets while doing laundry, he would dismiss my concerns, claiming they belonged to his brother, who had given them to him to hide from his own wife. This broke my heart, because it meant that Jason was being unfaithful to Lynn, whom I loved dearly. But it wasn't my place to interfere with their marriage, so I never said anything about it.

One evening, I returned home after finishing my shift to find the house empty. Oliva was at the sitter's place for the night, so I figured Tom and I could get out and do something. I called him to see where he was at, and a girl answered. I could hear him laughing as he grabbed the phone away from her.

"Yeah?"

It took me a few seconds to figure out what to say. "Who the fuck was that?"

He hung up.

I called back—probably fifty times, if I had to guess.

He ignored all my calls.

The shock and betrayal ignited a firestorm of emotion. My whole body was set ablaze as two years of my life went down the drain. Despite all the sacrifices I'd made for him— losing touch with friends, distancing myself from family, and sacrificing any kind of a social life—I found myself standing there like a fucking fool.

That was it. I was done. I'd put up with enough of his bullshit. I'd bent over backward, trying to mold myself into what I believed he wanted me to be, only to realize it would never be enough. I packed up mine things and Olivia's, and we were moved out and back to my mom's by morning.

Chapter 25

I waited at the bar as my date went to the bathroom. It was my first date in months, but I'd finally mustered the courage to dip my toes back into the dating pool. While the guy wasn't exactly my type, he was nice enough and met most of my criteria: he wasn't from the area, drove a Porsche, and seemed to be financially stable. Just as the bartender placed our drinks in front of our seats, I felt my phone buzz in my purse. I picked it up and was taken aback by the name that appeared across the screen.

It was Tom.

I hadn't talked to him since I moved out. I was still so mad at him for the pain he'd caused me, and I was finding it hard to forget the heartache he put me through. I couldn't believe he had the nerve to text me!

Who does he think he is, thinking he can just waltz back into my life as if nothing has happened?

Despite my efforts to resist, curiosity got the better of me, and I found myself reaching for my phone as my date excused himself to use the restroom. With a sigh, I opened the text. It contained just three words. I reread those words, unsure of how to feel about them. Before I could dwell on it further, my date returned, and I quickly tossed my phone into my purse.

I was determined to focus on the present moment. I set my phone face down on the bar, refusing to give in to the temptation to read his text until after my evening was over. I took a deliberate sip of my drink, allowing myself to become immersed in the conversation with my date. I silently promised to keep my attention where it belonged—on the person in front of me.

It didn't work.

Tom's message had disrupted my whole evening, triggering past emotions and bringing up unanswered questions. I went as far as kissing my date to distract myself from it all, but that didn't work either. I ended up making up an excuse as to why I had to go home early. My night was ruined.

I took a seat on the porch and lit a cigarette as I watched the taillights turn the corner. I sat there wondering what had prompted Tom to text me. While I'd never believed his relationship with the girl he'd cheated on me with would last, I'd never given much thought about what would happen once it inevitably fell apart. I took a drag of my cigarette and grabbed my phone out of my purse. My fingers hovered over the keys as I began typing a response, only to delete it and throw my phone back into my purse.

I stared up at the stars looking for the right answer, hoping they would spell out the perfect response to Tom's unexpected message. I took a deep breath as I reached back into my purse to retrieve my phone once more. I stood up and flicked my cigarette into the street, looking at the words I'd typed on the phone screen just before hitting Send:

I miss you too.

Chapter 26

It started with a phone call here and a text message there, followed by casual hanging out over a drink. I never directly asked Tom why he'd done what he did to me, but I did let him know that he was an asshole for doing it. My initial reluctance was broken down after all of the pleading for another chance. Before I knew it, we were back together.

Truthfully, I missed the stability and security he provided, something that I was unable to provide on my own. I promised myself to take it slow this time around, but in typical Holly fashion, my life just didn't work that way. Another argument with my mom left me feeling vulnerable, and when I reached out to Tom to vent, he stepped in like a knight in shining armor, offering his home as a refuge. Predictably, I fell for it and soon found myself moving in with him once again.

Things were better for a while. It didn't take long for me to fall back into the role of obedient girlfriend, bending over backward to make him happy. He continued with his past behavior, masking it behind his charm and ability to manipulate me into believing anything. We lived like this for three years before he decided to follow society's expectations and take the next step.

After a long, exhausting shift at work, I trudged through the front door, glad to be home. I could hear the kids playing in the back yard as I walked up to the kitchen table, untying my work apron. I set it on the table and made my way outside onto the deck, where Tom stood watching the kids play.

Irritable from waiting tables for rude customers all day, I shot down his idea of finding a sitter so we could go to dinner, even though he insisted. I was tired, yet I mostly didn't want to go because I didn't want to see the looks of disgust he made while watching me eat. He offered to take the kids up to his parents in Chicago so we could have the night to ourselves. I was getting slightly annoyed. I walked to the edge of the deck and leaned against the railing.

"Do you want this or not?"

"Do I want what—"

I turned around to see Tom holding a ring. A beautiful diamond ring.

I'm such an asshole.

I was completely caught off guard. I had no idea he was trying to take me out so he could propose to me. I had no idea he even wanted to marry me. I was stunned, so shocked that instead of saying yes, I apologized profusely for inadvertently ruining the moment. Then I said yes.

Every lingering insecurity I'd harbored about our relationship vanished into thin air at that moment. This was what it felt like to be chosen, and not just as a girlfriend, but as a partner for life. Not just that, but I would be the first of my sisters to get married. This would prove that I wasn't such a fuck-up after all.

Chapter 27

The bliss of being newly engaged didn't last terribly long. I found myself discovering more pictures of strange naked women, all of which Tom continued to claim were a mere joke sent to him by friends, all of which I continued to believe. Deep down I knew he was lying, but at this point in our relationship, I'd become so isolated and dependent on him that I had nowhere else to run to.

Instead, I found myself caught in the throes of insecurity and self-doubt. I began comparing myself to them: young, thin, big tits, and effortlessly beautiful—everything that I felt I wasn't. In my mind, I thought that this was the type of woman he wanted to look at, the type of girl he really wanted to be with. He and his brother always criticized their friends' wives, picking apart their appearance, commenting on their weight or the fact that their breasts weren't perfect after having four kids. Who's to say they weren't saying the same shit about me when I wasn't around? Maybe this was why he was so critical of how I dressed and always scrutinized my eating habits.

We would go out to eat and, after starving myself all day, I would get halfway through my meal, and he would look at me with disgust.

"Are you really going to eat all of that?"

I guess not.

Any time I ate he always watched me. I knew that I could only have a couple of bites and I would have to save the rest for when he wasn't around. I began having to eat in secret, finding it hard to control my hunger at times. My appetite was suppressed by the fear that any weight gain would lead him to seek out attention elsewhere. It planted the seeds of an enduring obsession with my weight and physical flaws, something that has come to be known as body dysmorphia, a relentless battle that continues to haunt me to this day.

The verbal assaults during our fights were serious blows to my self-esteem, each cruel word carved deep into my bones. He would brand me as "fat" and "ugly," only fueling my obsession to become what he wanted me to be. After being told these things for so long, you start to believe them. What I saw in the mirror was a distorted reflection of what people saw in real life. Looking at pictures of myself from that period, I can see how unhealthy I truly was.

Tom was offered an opportunity to take over the business he worked for, and with my help and encouragement, we made it a successful one. Money was flowing in hand over fist, and we did the smart thing and invested it right back into the business. This allowed us to grow—slowly at first, but after a few months, we found ourselves moving into a large warehouse with multiple employees, opening offices in different states.

Because of the felony on Tom's record, we decided to register the business under my name. I took charge of the administrative tasks while he oversaw operations in the warehouse. Initially, we made a solid and effective team, until

I came to realize that we weren't really a team at all.

One of his forms of control was withholding financial information from me, both in our business dealings and personal finances. He spent money recklessly, creating the illusion of financial stability, which was a stark contrast from my frugal habits and cautious approach to spending. I still found myself thrifting and buying whatever was on sale, just to save a few dollars. I wanted to build our financial security, not blow every dollar we had.

I was in the kitchen on my computer, wrapping up the workday, when he strolled in. The first thing that caught my eye was the shiny new Rolex on his wrist. I slammed my computer shut, obviously not thrilled that he'd gone and spent $10,000 on a watch for himself. A Cheshire Cat grin spread across his face, a sinister expression I often interpreted as his acknowledgment of what he'd done and the fact that there was nothing I could do about it.

I took a moment to compose myself. I could already hear his argument: "It's an investment," he would claim. Bullshit. I needed to find a way to take this situation by the balls. How could I make this work in my favor? And then it hit me: an investment for an investment.

"Fuck you. I'm getting a boob job, then."

He had no argument.

I called the next day and made an appointment for a consultation.

Chapter 28

We got married in Las Vegas at Caesars Palace. My three closest friends came in place of my sisters, who weren't able to make it. As we sat in the bridal suite sipping champagne, I began to wonder if I was making a big mistake. Before I could even think it through, they were calling me to the altar.

I stood at the doors to the chapel, feeling the weight of indecision pressing down on me. This was my last chance to run. My eyes darted from left to right, seeking the best escape route out of there. I could hear the music from behind the doors, signaling my entrance, and the doors began to creak open. It was too late; I'd missed my chance. With everyone's eyes on me, I walked slowly down the aisle toward the altar where Tom was waiting.

He looked good in his custom tailored, $1000 suit, while my $200 dress from eBay seemed to disguise its modest price tag. We stood in front of the altar, hand in hand. I watched him as he recited his vows, trying to detect any hint of deceit, but the sound of my pounding heart drowned out his words, echoing loudly in my ears.

Shit. Now it's my turn.

Just repeat what this guy tells you to say.

Breathe in. Breathe out.

I got through the first few lines, repeating every word robotically.

"Will you love and respect… " the preacher recited. Blah, blah, blah.

Respect? I never received any respect from Tom. I wasn't even allowed to have a bachelorette party, while he went out and had two bachelor parties for himself! But I was expected to respect him? I wasn't even sure if I loved him, yet here I was. I found it amusing and began to chuckle. I quickly gathered myself and continued, repeating the vows word for word, my focus on controlling my quivering legs.

We all walked down to the piano bar to have a celebratory cocktail. I grabbed my drink off the bar and walked over to where Tom was seated, looking at his phone. As I came up behind him, I could see what he was looking at so intently on his phone screen.

A picture of some young woman. Naked.

We'd been married for five minutes.

I slapped him upside the head and slammed my drink on the table before storming off, leaving our guests questioning the sudden turn of events. He chased after me, laughing at my reaction as if I were overreacting. He continued to explain that it had been sent as a joke from Tommy, since he couldn't be there. I was making a big deal out of nothing. I knew he was lying, but what could I do? We'd just committed to spending the rest of our lives together. There was no turning back now.

I found myself once again forced to believe him, pushing aside my anger as we returned to the piano bar to rejoin our guests. The celebration continued into the night, with Tom becoming so intoxicated that he stumbled back to our room long before I even considered heading back. It was a far cry from the traditional wedding night that I'd imagined and, wanting a non-traditional wedding, I guess in a twisted way you could say I got what I wanted.

Back home, we threw a big reception where all our family could join and celebrate our union. It was a more traditional affair compared to our wedding ceremony. We had dinner, cake, and a DJ spinning music, making it quite the party, enjoyed by everyone—especially Tom. Unfortunately, he ended up getting excessively drunk yet again, spending a good portion of the night in the bathroom, vomiting red wine all over his expensive suit. His dad and brother had to take him home while I carried on with the festivities. Needless to say, my hopes for a second chance at consummating our marriage were dashed once again.

If I'd known then what I know now, I would have left that piano bar and annulled the entire thing.

Chapter 29

We moved into a house in a nice neighborhood, surrounded by friendly neighbors and plenty of children for our kids to play with. We took care of the practicalities of married life, merging bank accounts and taking out life insurance on each other, at Tom's request, to ensure our future security. The business was going strong, and we were working every day, morning and night, with no weekends off and no holidays. It was a small price to pay for the life we were living.

I began to sink into a state of depression. I longed for the companionship of my old friends, but I'd formed new connections with the ladies in the neighborhood. We would gather in the evenings, sharing drinks and conversation in someone's driveway. Although these new friends were older than me, Tom approved of them. At least he didn't think they were whores like my old friends.

My new friends suggested going to a local bar one night. Instead of simply agreeing to join them, I felt compelled to ask for permission first. I felt like I was fifteen asking my parents to hang out with a boy for the first time. Except I was twenty-eight years old, asking my husband for permission to hang out with our neighbors.

I promised not to be out long, and he okayed it. I was so excited and got ready in a hurry. I was in the bathroom putting my makeup on when he walked in and decided to pick a fight with me. He wanted to know why I was putting makeup on to go to a bar, thinking that my intention was to get attention from other men, which wasn't the case.

I assured him my intention was to enjoy a night out with my friends. I closed my makeup and started placing it back in its designated drawer, when an explosion from underneath sent it all flying into the air, sending it crashing to the floor. Tom had kicked the drawer right out of its tracks, and my makeup lay crumbled amid splinters of wood.

I turned to him, struggling to hold back tears. I couldn't comprehend why he'd reacted so violently. Gritting my teeth, I began to gather the scattered makeup, salvaging what I could, all while he remained unmoved. I stood up and washed the makeup off my hands. I wasn't going to let him ruin this for me.

It's unfortunate how things changed with my neighbor friends. Tom suddenly labeled them as whores, and I was forbidden from spending time with them. Looking back, I should have recognized this as a warning sign. His accusations mirrored his own actions, yet I chose to turn a blind eye because I didn't want to acknowledge the truth.

He did something like this anytime I wanted to do anything with anyone. It got to the point where I would have to plead and shed tears just to see my old friends, even for a brief moment. Eventually, he would relent, seeing as this gave him an opportunity to go do whatever the hell it was that he was out doing.

Despite my instincts screaming that something was off, I tried to quiet them down, convincing myself I was just being paranoid. The business required him to be on the road a lot, and even though he'd fucked around on me a couple of times before, we were married now; surely things were different.

Growing up in a household shattered by divorce instilled in me a profound resistance to the idea of ending a marriage. Olivia finally had a father figure in her life, along with a stepsister she genuinely got along with. I was determined to rise above the pain I'd witnessed and experienced. My commitment to our vows was unwavering, even if I chuckled when I uttered them. To me, divorce wasn't an option. I'd told him that the only way he was getting out of this marriage was in a body bag or a casket, and I meant every word of it.

Chapter 30

We were coming up on our one-year anniversary when I got a call from a nurse at the ER, saying that Tom had just been in an accident on his motorcycle. I rushed to the hospital to find him lying in a bed hooked up to morphine after suffering from severe road rash and a concussion. When I questioned him about the accident, all he could offer was that he hit gravel and lost control of his bike. I noted the absence of his Rolex, which I assumed had fallen off during the fall.

The police arrived and began their questioning. Tom struggled to recall how he'd reached the hospital and where the accident had taken place. His apparent memory lapse struck me as odd. Finally, he managed to recollect something, claiming that an elderly woman had stopped after witnessing the crash and had offered him a ride. He provided the officers with a road name, and they departed to search for his motorcycle and the missing Rolex.

After several hours of searching, the officers returned empty-handed. Despite scouring the road and its adjacent streets, they found neither the motorcycle nor the missing watch. Their suspicion toward Tom grew, but lacking evidence, they concluded their investigation and departed after filing a report. However, my own suspicion lingered, unsettled by the unresolved circumstances surrounding the accident.

Tom was knocked out on the drugs administered by the doctors, giving me an opportunity to access his phone. It was locked, of course. I didn't know the code. I tried a few combinations but fearing the risk of getting locked out of it, I set it back on the table. Bothered, I leaned back in my chair. He was lying. I knew it; I just couldn't prove it.

He was home later that night and I tended to him, helping him with washing and applying ointment to his wounds before bandaging them the best I could. He stayed in bed, in and out of sleep from the medication they'd given him. When he was awake, he was on his phone, texting someone I was sure he shouldn't have been texting, but I went about my business playing the role of loving, attentive wife.

The motorcycle miraculously reappeared in the garage not long after the accident. When I questioned Tom about its sudden reappearance, he claimed that a neighbor across the street had found it and placed it in their garage for safekeeping. Additionally, he filed an insurance claim for his missing Rolex and received a reimbursement check of approximately $10,000—money that I never saw.

At this point, I'd learned not to ask any questions. Any time I did, he would react as if I were insulting him. Innocent inquiries would be twisted into accusations of disloyalty, leaving me scrambling to prove my devotion. I found it best to leave things be. The less I knew, the better

Chapter 31

Our one-year anniversary consisted of me spending the night alone, eating stale wedding cake from our wedding reception that was kept in our freezer, while Tom worked late into the night. Despite the loneliness I felt, I was glad to be alone, eating cake without feeling guilty for once. I didn't let our ruined anniversary dampen my mood; instead, I focused on the next week's tasks.

I got to the office early to wash the walls and prepare them to be painted. I gathered all my supplies in the center of the room and readied myself to begin. Pouring the paint into the tray, I picked up the roller, only to notice that my wedding ring was still on my finger. I set the roller down and walked over to where I'd left my purse. I took my ring off and put it in the side pocket of my purse, zipping it, making sure it was secure and safe before getting back to work.

After three exhausting days of painting every room, my hand and arm throbbed, and my vision blurred from the repetitive motion. Dropping the roller into the tray after the final stroke, I sank into a nearby chair, surveying the rooms with a sense of accomplishment. As I sat, I massaged my tired hand, glancing down at it. Paint smudged my fingers, evidence of the work

I'd done. For the past three days, my ring had remained safely tucked away in my purse to avoid getting paint on it. Paint was splattered all over my arms and sprinkled in my hair. I needed to go home and shower. I would put my ring back on after that.

I took a nice long shower once I got home. I was exhausted. I'd planned on putting my pajamas on and going right to bed. I'd just got done brushing my hair when I realized I'd forgotten to put my ring back on. I headed to the kitchen, where my purse was sitting on the counter, and unzipped the pocket where I'd kept it for safekeeping.

I dug my hand to the bottom of the pocket, fishing for the circular band, reaching deep into the corner.

And then into the other corner, frantically feeling for anything resembling a ring in the pocket.

I probed each corner, each crevice, but found nothing. With growing desperation, I turned the pocket inside out, hoping against hope that the ring had somehow slipped from its confines. I checked the seam for a hole, thinking that maybe it fell out and into the larger part of the purse. I took out every item, one by one, placing them in a pile next to my purse until it was completely empty.

And still no ring.

It was gone.

Vanished.

Panic surged through me. Did it fall out of my purse in the car? I bolted to the garage. I tore through the car with desperate urgency, flipping floor mats and wrenching seats forward and back in a frantic search. Still nothing. Dread gripped me tightly as I faced the grim reality: I'd lost something invaluable, and the looming prospect of facing Tom's anger filled me with dread. He was going to kill me.

Frantically, I slipped on a pair of slippers, snatched my keys, and dashed back to the car. It had to be at the office. It must have fallen out there somehow.

But how?

I raced to the office, searching every room I'd been in, scouring every nook and cranny where I might have left my purse.

Nothing.

I felt lost and overwhelmed, unsure of what to do or how to face Tom with the news. With a heavy heart, I headed to the gravel parking lot, the only place I hadn't searched. Armed with a flashlight from the warehouse, I combed through the gravel on my hands and knees, the light quivering as I desperately hoped it would catch the glimmer of my diamond ring. But it never did. Tears streamed down my face as I scooped up handfuls of gravel, sifting it through my fingers until only dust remained. Exhausted and defeated, covered in gravel dust and tears, I sank onto the ground just as Tom's work van pulled up.

FUCK.

I desperately hoped Tom wouldn't notice me, or perhaps if I ignored him, he would ignore me too. I continued my search, sifting through the gravel. My hopes were dashed when he got out of the van and approached me while I continued my futile search.

"What's wrong with you? What are you doing?"

There it was, the dreaded question.

I paused. I'd lost an $15,000 ring. I couldn't even tell him what happened because I didn't know. I would have to endure another tirade over my incompetence, listen to him telling me how stupid I was and how I was good for nothing. I would have to beg for forgiveness for days on end. It would become another weapon in his arsenal to belittle and control me.

I remained frozen on all fours, clutching the flashlight, until I couldn't hold back the flood of tears any longer. Collapsing onto my knees, I buried my face in my hands, smearing the gravel dust on my cheeks, trying to swallow my uncontrollable sobs.

Tom came over and attempted to consol me, asking me what the problem was.

I had to confess. "It's gone."

"What's gone?"

"My ring. It's missing. I can't find it anywhere."

Through my uncontrollable sobs and quivering voice, I recounted how I'd placed it securely in the side pocket of my purse. How I'd searched everywhere—our home, the office, even my car—but the ring was nowhere to be found. I braced myself for the anger that was to follow, but instead he hugged me and laughed.

"It's okay, we'll get you a new one."

Wait.

That was it?

His unexpected reaction left me speechless. There were no eruptions of anger, no violent outbursts, no shattering of objects—just a calm demeanor that I found unsettling. Looking back, I should have realized that something wasn't right, given his typically volatile temper. Yet in that moment, I was simply relieved not to have faced his wrath. Still, the weight of guilt and anxiety lingered for days afterward.

Chapter 32

It was a busy day at the office. The phone was ringing off the hook, and halls were filled with chatter from our employees. I was in the middle of activating an order when my computer crashed. I hastily jotted down the information I needed and ran down the hall to Tom's office to use his computer. With a quick movement of the mouse, I expected the screen to awaken, ready for my input. However, what greeted me next was wholly unexpected.

The screen woke up, all right. On it was a picture of a naked girl.

A girl who wasn't me.

My temperature began to rise, and I could feel my blood starting to boil. I quickly minimized the picture, only to find more images. All of the same girl.

I pulled my phone out and took pictures of what I'd found— evidence of what I'd suspected all along. I sat in his desk chair studying each picture before beginning my investigation. She was pretty, but she wore too much makeup and her teeth were fucked up. I could tell her tits were fake, not that I cared to see them. Yet there they were, plastered all over my husband's computer screen.

I logged into our cell phone account and started scanning through his incoming and outgoing messages and phone calls. One number stood out, appearing more frequently than any others, even mine. I scribbled it down on a piece of paper and shoved it into my pocket. I deleted the pictures I'd found on his computer just before locking up his office and quietly left the building.

I sat in my car, clutching the slip of paper with the mysterious phone number in one hand while my cell phone rested heavily in the other. The impulse to call and confront whoever answered surged within me, but deep down, I already knew it was her. Setting the paper aside, I opted to text Tom instead, my anger clouding my thoughts. With trembling fingers, I scrolled through the explicit photos I'd captured, my breathing becoming heavy. I pulled up Tom's name in my contacts, attached the images and hit send, my heart pounding in my chest.

CARE TO EXPLAIN WHAT THE FUCK THESE ARE?

My phone rang almost immediately after I hit the Send button.

Where did you get those?

It wasn't even a question. He knew exactly where I got them. And I had no problem telling him how I'd stumbled upon them before hanging up and dialing the mysterious number on the piece of paper.

The phone rang twice before a woman answered. "Hello?"

"Who is this?"

"Stacey. Who is this?"

"What the *fuck* is going on with you and *my husband*?"

She went silent.

"You do know that kids are involved, right?"

She hung up after that.

I sped home, unable to control my tears. I could no longer deny that my life was a lie.

All the times he'd told me he loved me, he was lying. The relationship I'd worked so hard on was based on lies.

I didn't know what was true and what was a lie anymore.

I'd given up my life for him.

My friends. My family.

I put so much pressure on myself to make him happy.

And what did I get in return?

Nothing.

Nothing but lies, deceit, and betrayal.

Chapter 33

I sat in the corner of the deck clutching my phone. Tom's barrage of calls had ceased, giving me an opportunity to search for an attorney online. I dialed the first number that popped up.

Through sobs, I explained my situation to the attorney who picked up. I swear I could hear the dollar signs spinning in her eyes the minute I mentioned our lucrative business. I hung up the phone, promising to call back and make an appointment once I was ready.

I wanted to leave, but I had nowhere to go. Tom had effectively cut me off from all of my friends and even my family. He'd made me so reliant on him to control me. He knew I had the ability to take half of what we had, and it was in his best interest to try to resolve this situation we now found ourselves in.

I thought it was best that we take some time apart. We decided not to rush into divorce proceedings but opted for a trial separation instead. I would find my own place and during this hiatus, we would reassess our priorities and desires. It felt absurd to even consider such a step just a little over a year into our marriage. Tom didn't want this initially and only agreed to it under the condition that he help me find a place to stay—a subtle yet unmistakable assertion of his control over the situation.

I found a condo not too far from the house, and Tom helped me move my belongings in. We split up the furniture without any arguments, and he was to deliver my elliptical at a later date. I unpacked everything and set up Olivia's room and mine while I listened to music. As I unpacked and arranged my belongings, I couldn't help but feel a sense of contentment despite the underlying sadness. Being in my own space brought a newfound sense of happiness.

I was happy to be away from him.

We went about our lives with normalcy for a few weeks. Tom had promised to cut things off with the mistress, but I came to find out that didn't happen. I didn't understand why he didn't want a divorce. Did he expect us all to be one big happy fucking family? It became painfully clear that reconciliation was never his intention. It wasn't me he couldn't let go of; it was his control over me he couldn't let go of.

I finished signing the papers for my attorney to file with the court requesting a dissolution of marriage. Before I left, I asked her if they could tell me when he would be served the papers, and she told me that they never know when they do it. But not to worry, I would know when the day came. Unsure of what to make of this, I eventually understood its meaning when the day arrived.

After assigning the day's jobs to the installers and reminding them to provide me with their estimated time of arrival at the first job site, I settled into my desk chair and sifted through my emails for any urgent matters. I had to make sure I was gone before Tom arrived. It was only a matter of time before he received the divorce papers, and I anticipated his reaction would be explosive.

I kept checking the clock, making sure I was good on time. I had approximately seven minutes before he would arrive, so I had to hurry. I gathered all my papers and put them in my bag before giving the receptionist one last task to complete before the end of the day. I'd just gone back to my computer to shut it down when Tom appeared in the doorway.

He stood there with a stack of papers in his hand, waiting for the room to clear.

"We need to talk," he said.

My heart stopped.

I stared at my blank computer screen. I'd begged my attorney to let me know what day he was going to be served but unfortunately, she was unable to do so. All she was able to tell me was that once he got them, I would know. And she was right.

"If you want to talk, you can call my attorney."

I sprang to my feet, grabbed my bag, and pushed through the doorway past him as I hurried to my car. His voice trailed behind me, urging me to stop and talk to him, but I couldn't. I knew this wasn't going to end well, and I had to get out of there as fast as possible. I got in my car, tossing my bag on the passenger seat as I shut the door, and started the engine.

Tom loomed outside my car window, bellowing furiously just before he started pounding on the glass. I threw the car into Reverse, trying to get him away from me without running him over as I backed out of my parking spot. When I slowed to a stop just before switching gears, I heard the back driver's side door open.

SHIT.

Before I knew it, his hand came from behind me, tightening around my neck. Reacting instinctively, I threw the car into Drive and slammed the gas pedal to the floor. Gravel sprayed, pelting the side panels of my car as I fishtailed out of the parking lot. His grip tightened, his determination evident as he struggled to keep pace beside the car before ultimately having to let go. Gasping for air, I brought the car to a halt a short distance away. Moments passed as I tried to collect myself, but my brief pause was interrupted. In the rearview mirror, I spotted his car rounding the corner, hurtling toward me. Without hesitation, I accelerated, careening through streets, disregarding red lights and stop signs in a desperate attempt to evade him. Yet he persisted in pursuing me. Fumbling in my purse, I managed to retrieve my phone and dialed 911.

My hysterics made it hard for the dispatcher to decipher what I was saying, but when they finally were able to make out the words, they instructed me to head to the police station where officers would be waiting. I stayed on the phone with them until I arrived. I was greeted by about five officers as I pulled up and parked. One came over to my car to assess my condition. As the others approached, Tom's car careened into the parking lot. He hastily parked his car and ran up to the officers, insisting they arrest me for running over his foot.

Judging by the expressions on their faces, they didn't believe him for a second.

"For someone who just had their foot run over, you seem to be able to run just fine."

They handcuffed him and escorted him inside for questioning. I remained in my car as the other officers consoled and calmed me. I recounted the events leading up to the altercation, explained that he'd just been served divorce papers, and about the confrontation at our office. They gave me the option to file a police report and press charges, but I knew that would only make Tom angrier and more likely to seek revenge. I felt I had no choice but to dismiss the whole incident and pray that he would leave me alone from here on out.

Chapter 34

Things between Tom and me settled down a few weeks later. My friend Emma and I decided to head to a local diner for some food after our night out at the bar. We'd taken a seat and were looking over the menu when I heard my name being called from across the restaurant. It was my old neighbors.

We left our booth and joined them at their table, exchanging stories about our night out. My phone buzzed continuously, but I chose to ignore it. Tom had been texting me throughout the night, telling me he missed me and he wanted me to come back home. I was tired of him toying with me. I finally opened my phone to clear the messages, unable to hide my facial expression, giving myself away that something was bothering me.

"Is that Tom?"

I looked up, trying not to appear bothered by the question. "Yes, he's been texting me all night, begging me to come over."

My old neighbors glanced at each other before looking back at me.

"Why would he want you to come over when she's there?" one of them asked.

Excuse me? Did you just say what I think you said?

I looked at Emma, who was already reaching for her purse. "Wanna go for a ride?"

"You bet your ass I do."

I turned down the music as we pulled up in front of the mailbox of my former home, spotting a strange SUV in the driveway. The neighbors hadn't lied about her being there. Why in the hell would he be trying to get me to come over when she was already here? I sat there, squeezing the steering wheel with both hands, staring straight ahead. Emma was saying something, but I couldn't hear her. I just sat there staring, controlling my breath.

I reached for the door handle. "I'll be right back."

I stepped out of my car and onto the driveway, still attempting to control my breathing, when a sense of calm came over me. That's when my peripheral vision began to turn red, until it consumed my entire field of vision. What happened next was a blur.

I kicked off my red high heels and marched right up to her SUV, using them to smash her car windows. I beat them against the glass as hard as I could. When I saw that I wasn't doing the damage I intended, I took aim at the side mirrors, smashing them and breaking them off. I didn't stop there. I took hold of the windshield wipers and ripped them off, throwing them to the ground. I grabbed my heels and headed to the front door, where I hurled them at the glass with the full intention of breaking it. When they didn't do the trick, I began pounding on the door with my fists so hard that my hands went numb, but I didn't care.

I was yelling at the top of my lungs, screaming for Tom to come out and for her to show her face. It was 3:00 in the morning, and I didn't give a shit who heard me. I could see through the glass on the door the shadow of a body coming up the basement stairs. I continued pounding on the door with all my might.

Tom flung the door open, shocked to see me. I stood there, heaving with rage, as he began to laugh. I charged at him, my voice a thunderous roar.

"You mother fucker! How dare you? Who the fuck do you think you are?!"

I looked past him—and there she was. In the hallway, just outside what used to be our bedroom, with her arms folded, wearing her pajamas and a smirk that mocked me like I was some sort of fool.

Me.

The fool.

That FUCKING whore.

I shifted my aim to her.

"Do you know what he's doing while you're sleeping? You fucking piece of shit! Do you know he still tells me he loves me? Do you know he still tells me he misses me? And he wants me back? You fucking White Trash whore!"

At this point he scooped me up, restraining my thrashing body, and carried me outside onto the front lawn. Despite his efforts to calm me, my rage persisted. He eventually released me, but I continued to lash out, hitting him and screaming in fury. I don't know who I wanted to hurt more—him or the bitch inside. Seeing that his attempts to calm me down weren't working, he finally let me go as I continued on my warpath.

Emma had gotten out of the car by then, joining the chaos. I could see her in the doorway of the house, throwing miscellaneous items outside. Shoes littered the front lawn. She didn't know whose they were, but she had to do something to help me. The whore approached her and asked her what she was doing, to which she bluntly responded with a solid, "Fuck you!" before coming to my aid and pulling me to the car.

We sped off. I was hot, my anger still simmering inside me like a blazing inferno. My shoes were thrown in the back seat, and Emma's laughter filled the car, contagious and freeing. I was barefoot, liberated, and unbound. I glanced at her, the events of moments ago still a blur through the haze of fury. A wave of laughter overtook me as well. It was a release, a realization that I'd finally let my emotions take the reins, refusing to take his shit any longer. For the first time, I'd stood up for myself, and in that moment, I felt a sense of pride.

He texted me not long after we left, saying that the whore wouldn't press charges on me for damaging her car. I texted back my favorite two words:

Fuck you.

Chapter 35

I would see Tom at the office, where he tried to charm and manipulate me for his benefit in court, but I wasn't having it. It wasn't but two weeks after I'd confronted him that I discovered his mistress had moved into our house. Well, that didn't take long. When he realized that his usual tricks weren't working on me any longer, it made him angry. This was when the threats began.

He began stalking me while I was out with my friends, sending me texts with pictures of me he'd taken or describing the outfit I had on, implying how easy it would be to snatch me up in the parking lot. Determined not to let it bother me, I stood my ground. I threatened to get the police involved, just like I had when he was served the divorce papers, and that got him to back off temporarily. Even so, any time I went anywhere, I was always looking over my shoulder. I always made sure I was with a group of people.

I found myself drinking almost daily, using it as my coping mechanism for the turmoil in my life. It was also the only thing the people I was hanging around with wanted to do, so it worked out. I was still working for the business, opting to do so from home so I didn't have to see Tom and risk another confrontation. Our divorce proceedings were still ongoing, with the complexities of business arrangements and asset division adding to the strain.

I would send Olivia to her babysitter's house for the weekend and go out with my new friends. We would hop around to all the bars in town, seeking out the liveliest crowds and the best tunes. In a short span, I forged numerous new friendships and even reconnected with Christy. I was thankful that she understood the situation I was in and an explanation wasn't necessary.

One weekend, Christy and I were heading out to meet up with the rest of the crew. I'd been single for about two months now. Not only had Tom swiftly moved his mistress into our house, but he'd also gotten her pregnant shortly after.

We'd just arrived at the bar and had squeezed our way to the front to get a drink. I found myself pressed shoulder to shoulder with someone I recognized from high school. He was attractive, with a tan complexion and muscular arms that caught my eye as he placed his credit card on the bar to open a tab. I decided I was going to strike up a conversation with him; I just needed to wait for the perfect moment.

"Hey, I like your watch."

Idiot.

Why am I like this? I asked myself, mentally kicking myself for my lackluster pickup line. *Hey, I like your watch? Really, Holly? That's the best you could do?* Despite my cringe-worthy attempt, it seemed to break the ice. We ended up chatting for most of the night, and he even tagged along with my friends and me to another bar where it was quieter and we could converse more easily.

As the night drew to a close, I made up my mind. I was

going to make a move and invite this guy—I'll call him Paul for the sake of the telling—back to my place. After all, Tom had already moved on, so why couldn't I? I hadn't been with anyone besides Tom for the past six years, while he'd been with who knew how many people—way more than I cared to know about. My inner pep talk continued as we walked out to our cars and finally, I mustered up the courage to ask him if he wanted to come over to my condo.

He did.

I glanced at my rearview mirror to ensure I could see Paul's headlights as I turned into my subdivision and pulled into my driveway. He followed suit, parking in the drive as I pulled into the garage. After closing the garage door and locking it behind us, we entered the kitchen. I offered to make us a drink, but he grabbed the glasses from my hands and placed them on the counter. Then he took hold of my hands and suggested that I lead him to the bedroom instead.

Chapter 36

I bolted upright in bed, startled by what sounded like a freight train plowing through my kitchen. It didn't take me long to piece together what was happening.

"Fuck!"

I was in nothing but my birthday suit.

Paul was also completely nude, still asleep next to me.

The lingering effects of last night's drinks were still coursing through my system. In an instant, adrenaline surged as I grasped the gravity of the situation. I began to violently shake the naked guy next to me awake, but he was out cold from our long night of drinking and sexcapades.

In rushed Tom, his face contorted in anger.

He stormed into the bedroom and delivered a powerful blow to Paul's jaw, startling him awake. Reacting swiftly, the naked man leaped up, forced to engage in a struggle, managing to put Tom in a headlock as Tom attempted to retaliate with punches, his face mere inches from Paul's penis. The tension escalated until my guest eventually subdued Tom, forcing him to tap out and collapse to the floor. Amid the chaos, I screamed at them both, clutching a sheet in a futile attempt to cover myself. I demanded that Tom leave immediately while pleading with

Paul to depart for his own safety. Words of apology poured out of my mouth as I struggled to comprehend the unfolding madness.

As I escorted Paul to the door, my apologies echoing behind him, I watched him depart knowing that I would probably never see him again. The kitchen door frame leading to the garage was busted, the garage door itself was open. But how? Tom had secretly programmed his car to open my garage door when he'd delivered the elliptical weeks earlier, a detail I'd been entirely unaware of until now.

Standing there, still naked and vulnerable, I turned around, stepping on splintered wood, and headed back to the room where Tom was. He had no authority over me anymore. How dare he barge in here, wielding force and destruction while leaving his pregnant girlfriend at home! I was done being controlled by him. I stepped into the room with the intent to give Tom a piece of my mind but instead, I came head to head with the devil.

He rushed me the minute my foot crossed into the room, pinning me against the wall by my throat. He lifted me off the floor until my toes could barely touch the carpet. My hands clawed at his, and my legs thrashed in every direction, trying to find some solid ground. The fire in his eyes burned black as he spewed venomous insults at me.

"You dirty fucking whore! You're nothing but a fucking slut."

He threw me to the floor where I tried to catch my breath, kicking me before ripping me up by my hair and forcefully guiding me into the bathroom. With a violent shove, he sent me tumbling to the shower floor as he commanded me to turn the water on and wash myself. Trembling with fear, I did as I was told, scared at what would happen if I didn't obey.

He loomed over me, watching as I rinsed with soap and water, my body shaking. Without warning, he seized my arm and yanked me out of the shower, leaving it to run, and forcibly pulled me back into the bedroom, flinging me onto the bed.

I knew what was going to happen next.

I pleaded with him.

I cried for him to stop.

I tightened my body, trying to close myself off.

I struggled against his weight; his shoulder pressed hard into the side of my face. My arms, trapped under his chest, were unable to push him off. I was pinned in such a way that I couldn't move. I squeezed my eyes shut and tried to pretend it wasn't happening. I tried to block out his vile words, calling me a fucking whore, a fucking slut, and if I wanted to be a fucking whore, then he would treat me like a fucking whore. I begged silently for it to end and finally, after what felt like an eternity, it did.

He put his jeans back on, buttoning them while looking at me up and down. I lay curled up in a ball, my tears concealed the best I could. I didn't dare show any signs of weakness. He finally put his shirt on and walked to the door, where he stopped briefly.

"No one will ever believe you."

Chapter 37

I lay there crying, cocooned in my sheets. unmoving until the distant growl of his car engine confirmed that he was leaving. I got up and ran to the broken door to make sure he was gone. He was. I ran into the still-running shower and got in it, the water since gone cold. I turned the hot water on all the way and began scrubbing, desperate to cleanse myself of his touch.

Scrubbing.

Washing… until I couldn't bear the cold water any more, forcing me to shut it off. I slumped to the shower floor. No amount of scrubbing could remove the stain he'd left on me. I couldn't wash away the dirtiness of what had just happened to me. He'd reduced me to the very labels he hurled at me: a dirty whore, a dirty slut. And I felt every bit of it.

The sound of a car pulling up in my driveway sent a shiver of dread through my body. The metallic clinks of tools reverberated through the air, suggesting someone was tampering with the recently damaged door. I didn't even bother to get up to see what was going on. I lay there, pretending to be dead, like I hoped to be, until the noises stopped and the car left.

I went to a really dark place after that. My movements were mechanical, only driven by the need to fulfill my responsibilities as a parent. It wasn't until I noticed the repaired door, a feeble attempt to erase the evidence of his intrusion, that I realized it must have been Tom that day. For almost two weeks, I remained confined to my bed, neglecting basic needs like eating and hygiene. Alcohol flowed steadily through my veins. I existed only as a shell of a person, empty on the inside, floating around like a ghost as I made sure Olivia got to school and had a hot meal on the table.

Tom had called and texted numerous times since the incident. He fabricated a story about me being sick and told everyone at work not to contact me. I felt trapped in a web of deceit, unsure of what to do next. Technically, we were still married; how could I say that my husband had raped me? He was right. No one would believe me. Tom's words echoed in my mind, reinforcing my worst fears about how I would be perceived.

I lay in bed when my mom called to check on me. Each attempt to speak only led to more tears, until Mom's patience wore thin. Unaware of what I'd gone through, her sharp words pierced through the phone, urging me to get up off my ass and get my life together. The call ended and I continued to lie there.

She was right. Letting my depression consume me wasn't helping anyone, especially not Olivia. I kept replaying words of advice my sister had given me shortly after learning about the circumstances of my divorce: never settle. And yet that's precisely what I'd done. I was determined to never do that again. I had to get out of bed and face each day with a brave face. I would push past the pain and forget about the terrible thing that had happened. I just wished it was that easy.

As each day passed, I began to improve. However, the changes in my appearance were unsettling. I'd lost a significant amount of weight and now wore a size two jeans, which looked too small on my tall frame. Looking at pictures from that time, I now see that I appeared skeletal. Ironically, my current appearance mirrored what I'd once strived for, hoping to divert Tom's attention from other women who had caught his eye.

I would see him at work sometimes, but I left as quickly as I could to avoid having a panic attack. The mere sight of him made my body unravel, the memory of his actions pulsating through the fibers in my muscles. The sound of his voice was snake-like, a hiss of ill intentions, his words constricting my throat, stifling my words. I made every effort to steer clear of him, for the sake of my sanity.

His attempts to charm and manipulate me into getting his way with the division of assets fell flat. Frustrated, he resorted to threats, including sabotaging the business. I knew he wouldn't risk his only income source, so he turned his threats toward me, leveraging past actions to instill fear.

They started small, with the typical slashing of the tires, but quickly escalated to more serious threats, such as setting my condo on fire while Olivia and I were sleeping. The final straw came when he ominously declared over the phone, "They would never find your body."

In an attempt to conceal my terror, I snapped back, "They'd find my implants; they have serial numbers. So, fuck you," before hanging up. This chilling threat was my sign that I had to get out of there.

It was no longer safe for me to be living in town. I had to put as much distance between Tom and me as possible. His threat on my life felt too real to dismiss. So, I made the decision to move to Florida after our court date.

I started making arrangements and filing paperwork to prepare for the move. I just wanted the divorce to be finalized. I wanted nothing to tie me to him anymore. I agreed to walk away from everything—the house, the cars—and I settled for the bare minimum in terms of the business. It felt like I was giving up a lot, but none of it was worth risking my life.

Chapter 38

Within my new group of friends was a former friend from high school, Zack. I used to be friends with his ex-fiancée and a few of his ex-girlfriends. He was funny and immature, but I saw no harm in that. I knew he liked me, but I wasn't interested in any kind of relationship. I was still in the process of getting divorced and dating was the last thing on my mind.

I felt a mountain of pressure from everyone around me to date Zack. The problem was, I simply didn't view him in that light; to me, he was just a friend. Moreover, I'd reconnected with Paul—yes, the same guy from that memorable night—and we were spending time together again. Zack's disappointment became evident whenever he joined us, leading him to express his frustration by punching walls. Things between Paul and me fizzled out rather quickly, leaving Zack at my side to be my shoulder to cry on.

Initially, my plan to move to Florida involved a group of us, but as the time approached, it dwindled down to just Zack and me. He saw this as his ticket out of there and perhaps as an opportunity to trap me into a relationship. At this point, I didn't give a shit. He eventually wore me down, although I made it clear that I wouldn't officially be his girlfriend until my divorce was finalized. My primary focus was escaping this town, and if that meant going with him, then so be it. I was determined to make the most of it and, at the very least, give it a chance. With the U-Haul packed, his car in tow, and Olivia and me in my car, we bid farewell to Zack's parents and embarked on our two-day adventure down to the Sunshine State.

I found a job in a matter of days. A Monday through Friday, nine-to-five job, holidays and weekends off, and no work to be taken home. It was a fantastic setup. My colleagues, a diverse mix of people from various backgrounds and ages, quickly became a source of valuable local knowledge. They shared tips on the best places to visit, restaurants to try, and where to catch live music on weekends. Meanwhile, Olivia got enrolled in the nearby elementary school, and we smoothly settled into our new life.

Zack, on the other hand, took his time adjusting. While he had a small investment covering his share of the bills, it wasn't much beyond that. Most days, I would come home from work to him sitting at the computer in his underwear watching fishing videos online. Occasionally, he prepared dinner but when he did, he seemed to expect praise for his efforts, a similarity between him and my stepmom that I found rather off-putting.

It came as no surprise when Zack had to sell his BMW to secure some funds. He ended up purchasing the neighbor's truck, which turned out to be a decent vehicle. He maintained it well, and it remained in excellent condition. However, despite these changes, Zack still lacked the motivation to go find a job.

I was getting frustrated with him. I would work all week while he sat at home doing nothing productive. I began searching the Want ads for him, finding job listings that I thought suited him. I came across job listings that aligned with his interests, such as positions on fishing charter boats, something that I knew he liked to do. He went on a few working interviews but, unfortunately, they didn't pan out. Zack possessed a likable personality; he was capable of getting along with anyone, yet he never wanted to take orders from anyone. He only wanted to be his own boss, which was the reason why he didn't care to go get a job. It appeared he was content to rely on his limited funds, assuming I would take care of the rest.

Chapter 39

I received a text from a friend informing me that Tom and his mistress had gotten engaged. It wasn't shocking news; after all, he'd gotten her pregnant. I'd had a feeling it was just a matter of time. My friend also sent me a picture of their engagement photo, not that I cared to see it. At first, it looked like the typical engagement picture. But then I saw it. The moment I laid eyes on it, everything clicked into place.

She was wearing my ring.

MY FUCKING RING!

The ring that I thought I'd lost. No, no, wait, let me rephrase that. The ring that HE MADE ME THINK I'D LOST! That fucking piece of shit took my ring out of my purse and let me believe I'd lost it! He watched me sit there and cry, devastated that I'd lost the symbol of our love, when it was all part of his con! He filed an insurance claim on my ring and pocketed the money, money I never laid eyes on, money for a replacement ring I never got. No wonder he didn't get mad at me when I confessed that I'd lost it!

Between my ring and his watch, he scammed our insurance company out of nearly $25,000. Then it hit me: I recalled the life insurance policy he'd taken out on me and the ominous threat against my life that drove me to flee the state. Was I merely another pawn in his scheme? Did he plan to end my life and collect the life insurance payout so that he and his new bride-to-be could live happily ever after, until it was her turn?

My head flooded with questions as I pieced everything together. I had so much I wanted to say to him. And her. But why waste my time? Fuck them both. They could have each other. After I got over the initial shock and anger of this new revelation, I took the mature approach and put it behind me as best I could.

Returning home late after dinner and a few drinks with a friend, I opted to sleep on the couch to avoid sharing the bed with Zack. I'd grown to dislike his presence and began actively creating distance between us in an attempt to get him to break up with me, since I didn't have the balls to do it myself. After dozing off, I was awakened by Zack, waving my cell phone in my face, brazen with anger.

"Who you callin' 'Sweet Tits,' huh?"

It took me a second to comprehend what was happening. *Did this asshole really go through my phone?*

I sat up and ripped my phone out of his hands. "What the fuck is wrong with you?"

"Who's Sweet Tits?"

"It's you, you stupid fuck!"

It was the nickname I'd given him when talking with my work friends. Even though there was an innocent explanation for it, he didn't believe me, and frankly, I didn't care. My tolerance for his irrational behavior and stupidity had gone out the window. He had no justification for snooping through my phone. I hadn't done anything wrong or given him any reason to lash out at me like that.

Zack had built a reputation for himself with his elaborate social media posts ranging from conspiracy theories to tales of alien encounters and grievances against those he felt had wronged him. This time, I found myself at the receiving end of his finger-pointing tirades. Soon enough, I started receiving messages and phone calls from concerned friends and acquaintances, checking in on me after Zack's online rants about me. While I was fine, I'd reached my limit. Enough was enough.

Olivia and I had just finished eating dinner when Zack pulled up in the driveway. I was doing my best to avoid him when he was home, so I headed to the bedroom. He came inside, insisting that we have a conversation. I made it clear that I had nothing to say and continued to occupy myself with my phone. Well, I guess what I wanted didn't matter.

He started yelling at me, loud enough that Olivia intervened, yelling at him to stop yelling at her mom. Quickly, I ushered Olivia into my room and shut the door, locking it behind us for some privacy and safety. I turned the TV on, turning the volume up to drown out Zack's continued shouting from the other side of the door. Olivia sat in the bed watching TV and I sat on the edge of the bed, contemplating what I should do. I couldn't believe this was happening to me. Again.

I heard the door slam shut and Zack's truck peel out of the driveway I was glad he was gone, but I needed him to be gone for good. I began searching for apartments online, finding a couple that seemed promising. Unfortunately, it was the weekend, so I would have to wait until Monday to make inquiries.

Chapter 40

I had no idea what time Zack returned home; it must have been early in the morning. He slept in the guest bedroom on the other side of the house. I was just starting my day when my phone rang; it was my friend. What she had to say sent me storming over to the other side of the house in a fit of rage.

She'd been at the bar last night, where she ran into Zack. Apparently, Zack had befriended some really shady people, and they were blowing coke all night long. She knew this firsthand because he offered her some. He was out until the wee hours of the morning doing drugs. Nice.

I'd spent how many years keeping my daughter away from that shit, and here he was, some douche bag, bringing cocaine right up to my doorstep. That was fucking it.

I busted the guest room door open.

"Get the *fuck* out!"

He started laughing at me.

"You have *one* week to get the *fuck* out of here, or I will throw your shit in the canal, and you can go fetch it from there in your stupid motorized kayak, you fucking pansy!"

I slammed the door shut and immediately began packing his

belongings then and there. I was deadly serious. No amount of pleading or begging would sway my decision. Messing with me was one thing, but when it came to my child, there was no room for negotiation.

The next few days were interesting, to say the least. Zack reverted to childlike behavior, calling me names, posting excruciating long social media posts accusing me of being a cheater, gold digger, and what I learned to be his favorite word: narcissist. He even stooped so low as to message my sisters and my mom, threatening to report me to Olivia's school, all in a desperate attempt to coerce me into letting him stay.

To top it off, I received a call from his mother—yes, his own mother—who berated me for breaking up with her son. What grown ass man had his mother call and yell at their ex for breaking up with them? Only Zack did. It was pathetic. I told her exactly what he'd done, but she dismissed me as a liar. Since I wasn't obligated to stay on the phone, I hung up and blocked her as she proved to be just as crazy as him.

A few days later, I received a message from a girl on social media, asking me why Zack was wanting to fly her down there just to fuck her in my bed. It seemed Zack was getting rather creative in his attempts to get back at me for what he perceived as ruining his life. I apologized to her and briefly explained the situation, to which she didn't seem surprised. We both found the absurdity of it all amusing and shared a laugh.

Zack conveniently shifted the blame onto me for his inability to stay in Florida. It wasn't because he didn't have a job and proof of income for the apartments he was eyeing or because he was unable to afford a security deposit. His dream of living the Florida life came crashing down due to his own actions, yet he chose to place the blame squarely on me as he was forced to make his way back home to Indiana.

Due to Zack's inability to take accountability for anything in his life, he tied a rope around my name and dragged it through the mud. Fabricated stories about me in an effort to draw sympathy from anyone who would listen. Being that I wasn't there to defend myself, most people either believed him or saw it for what it was: just another pissed off Zack rant. I hoped for the latter; I never saw the point in defending myself against such nonsense. Those who truly knew me understood that his words held no truth.

I pressed forward with my life, focusing on my work, caring for Olivia, and enjoying the freedom of being single. When you're rendered powerless in a situation, you must trust that karma will eventually catch up and deliver the swift kick in the ass that will send the other people flying into the consequences of their own actions with no one to blame but themselves. The truth has a way of surfacing eventually, whether it's sooner or later. I simply had to remain patient, even if the opportunity didn't arise until years later.

Chapter 41

I started feeling homesick. While I loved Florida, I longed for the seasonal changes I'd grown up with. I was also debating on going back to college. I reached out to local colleges, gathering information on various programs. However, I was discouraged to learn that I was classified as an out-of-state student since I hadn't lived in the state for more than a year. I decided to look into the schools back home, to see if tuition would be more affordable. It was.

Something to consider.

I tried my hand at the Florida dating scene, but it was, well, weird. I talked to a few people but never actually went on any dates. Most of the people down there were visitors or tourists, not there for long. With each passing day, the prospect of moving back home became more appealing.

It was a scorching afternoon. Olivia had a few friends over for a swim, and I was at the sink doing dishes, keeping an eye on them through the window. My phone rang.

It was Justin, Bryan's brother. Justin was the type to text if it was something trivial; a phone call meant it was serious. I quickly dried my hands and answered.

"It's Bryan."

This was it.

It was the moment I'd been dreading, the one I knew I would eventually have to face.

Justin proceeded to share some troubling news with me. Bryan had landed himself in trouble and ended up in jail. While this didn't come as a complete surprise, what followed was beyond anything I could have anticipated. Bryan had sustained a severe injury while incarcerated and was now on life support. The details were unclear, but I was informed that he'd broken his neck and the prognosis was grim. The doctors didn't hold out much hope for his survival. If he did survive, he would never be the same.

This was the moment that I'd been preparing for—the moment when I would have to explain to Olivia why her father and I weren't together, why I'd done everything in my power to keep her from him. I had to tell her the truth: that he'd chosen a life of drugs and crime over being her father. And now, I had to break the devastating news that he wasn't expected to survive.

I waited until Olivia's friends had left before sitting her down to break the news. There was no sugar coating it, so I spoke plainly and directly. As I delivered the information, Olivia, now in her preteens, bowed her head, and a single tear escaped her eye. I wasn't sure how she would react, but I braced myself for the worst.

"Can I go play now?"

This was precisely why I'd taken the actions I had, why I'd fought tirelessly to keep her safe. I'd anticipated that her first heartbreak would come from her father, and I'd done everything in my power to shield her from that pain. And it had worked. I gave her a big hug and kiss and let her continue playing.

A few days later, Bryan regained consciousness and was taken off life support. He underwent emergency surgery that left him paralyzed from the neck down and in need of round-the-clock care. While it was good news, it was still difficult for me to fully grasp. Despite his paralysis, I saw it as the best outcome for him. He could no longer harm himself, and I believed God had made sure of that.

Chapter 42

I'd made the decision to move back home to Indiana. After searching for apartments, I found one that would be available at the end of the school year. I almost had to pull Olivia out of school a week early but luckily, her teacher had plans to fly to Indianapolis the day after school ended and agreed to take her along. I coordinated with the family of one of her friends and her teacher, ensuring Olivia could complete her last week of school. Meanwhile, I used this time to arrange our new apartment and search for employment.

One good thing about moving is that it gives you the opportunity to get organized. With the entire house packed and ready to load onto the moving truck, I turned my attention to my box of files. I spent the evening sorting through them, labeling the folders and placing them back into the box in an orderly manner. When I left Tom, in my haste to leave the house, I'd grabbed the files from the general area where I remembered mine being. Little did I realize I'd also picked up a file that would unearth all the lies he'd ever told me. As I went through the files, I stumbled upon one with no label. I opened it to find what I now know to be Tom's permanent record.

I held in my hands Tom's presentence investigation report. I shit you not, this document spanned a whopping forty-four pages and covered arrests across five different states. Within its contents, I discovered the gritty truth of the man I'd once thought I knew.

He went by nine different aliases, some of which I recognized as belonging to his brothers and old friends he'd mentioned from his past. A staggering thirty-seven past arrests followed the first page that outlined his criminal profile. Details of each arrest were documented, ranging from car theft in Illinois to felony possession of a firearm, possession of a firearm by a convicted felon, battery charges in Florida, and a myriad of other disturbing run-ins with the law.

As it turned out, that felony charge wasn't the result of some legal loophole, like he claimed. The document provided a detailed account of the entire arrest. It described how he'd gotten caught chopping cars for parts and attempted to evade arrest by fleeing and hiding under a trailer. Law enforcement officers deployed dogs to track him down, leading to his discovery along with the arsenal of weapons he had in his possession.

Sitting on the floor, I poured over the pages one by one. When I finally reached the end, I set the papers in my lap and found myself lost in thought, staring into space. How was it possible that I'd spent six years with this man, yet not once did his family mention any of this to me? How was it that none of this ever came up in conversation, not even once?

Six years.

And I had no idea who I was married to.

With trembling hands, I carefully placed my newfound

treasure into a new file labeled "TOM" and tucked it safely into the box.

Chapter 43

I found a job as a bartender at an upscale restaurant downtown and shortly thereafter, I started working as a dental assistant in a local dentist's office. Meanwhile, I enrolled myself at the community college to take some prerequisite classes, still unsure of which career path to pursue but determined to forge a path toward a better future. While bartending brought in decent money, I recognized its limitations—it was a job I would likely have to do indefinitely since there were no retirement benefits or health benefits to speak of.

It didn't take long for Tom to discover that I was back in town. Despite having blocked him on every platform, his new cell phone number somehow managed to reach me via text message. While I can't recall the specific threat he sent this time, my response was the one that got him to shut up for good.

"So, when I call the police to report you, what name should I give… Tom? Or one of the nine other ones you like to use…"

He knew I knew.

Game over.

And just like that, he disappeared from my life for good.

It didn't take Zack long to discover that I was back in town either. In fact, I wouldn't have been surprised if Zack was the one who informed Tom of my return, considering he'd seemed to befriend him solely to get under my skin. Given that many of Zack's friends frequented the downtown bar scene where I worked, they likely reported back to him whenever they saw me behind the bar. This would lead to him showing up at my job with his friends, purposefully sitting at the bar to force me to wait on him.

Fine.

After serving him his drink, I made a point to completely ignore him.

He hated it. He talked as loudly as he could, trying to catch my attention with whatever preposterous stories that came out of his mouth. But he wasn't fooling me. Had he conveniently forgotten about all the lies he'd spread about me while I was away? Or about his offer to fly some woman down to Florida and pay her to sleep with him in my bed?

I certainly hadn't.

I placed his bill in front of him, silently signaling that it was time for him to leave. He laid out cash on the bar, and as I reached to collect it in order to return his change, he called a truce, insisting that I keep the change.

A fucking truce?

Like I was the one starting and talking shit. As if leaving me a generous tip could make up for the fact that he'd tarnished my reputation throughout town in an attempt to save his own skin. Not a chance, buddy. I took my tip, along with his change, and set it back in front of him.

"Keep your money; you need it more than me."

I would run into him when I went out with friends and every

time, he would drink in excess and act like a fool. He even went out of his way to sit next to me at the bar, prompting me to explain to him, in simple terms even a kindergartener could grasp, that we weren't friends. I made it crystal clear: We were not friends. I did not have to greet him, I did not have to acknowledge him. I even had Christy, a mutual friend, reinforce this message for me. But it seemed to fall on deaf ears.

Jenny—the girl Zack had propositioned on social media—and I decided to meet up and chat one afternoon. We chose a restaurant on the downtown square and settled at the bar, sipping on margaritas as we exchanged stories about our experiences with Zack. We couldn't help but laugh as we both reached the conclusion that he was an even bigger idiot than we'd initially thought. We heard the door open and the chatter of a group of guys approaching the bar. Glancing over, I spotted Zack, his face drained of color, staring in shock at the sight of Jenny and me getting along famously.

He instantly became uncomfortable as he witnessed himself getting caught in his own bullshit. Resorting to his usual theatrics—loud talking, downing shot after shot—he put on a pitiful display. It was quite a sight to behold, really. Jenny and I found the whole spectacle amusing and opted to sit back and enjoy the Zack show from a distance.

We decided to leave and head to another bar, one with a patio where we could enjoy the outdoor atmosphere. As luck would have it, we bumped into another mutual friend who ended up joining us. While chatting, we noticed Zack and his friends heading up the stairs with a group of girls to an apartment above one of the restaurants downtown. I hadn't been certain which restaurant he lived above until that moment. Regardless, we carried on with our evening, not letting Zack's presence dampen our spirits.

Shortly after they disappeared into his apartment, he reappeared on the balcony with a young woman, engaged in a loud and obnoxious conversation. He was all over this poor girl, seemingly trying to provoke jealousy in me, or perhaps Jenny, or maybe just anyone who would pay attention. But all he succeeded in doing was making me feel nauseous. I'd had enough. I just wanted to enjoy the evening with my new friend. As he continued pulling his shit, I cupped my hands around my mouth and aimed my words right at him.

"Have fun in the Cialis palace!"

The entire table burst into laughter as I raised my glass and toasted the air in his direction. This wasn't a lie; he'd blamed me for wasting his precious erectile dysfunction pills because I never wanted to be intimate with him. After learning a little bit about him, do you blame me?

He eventually started seeing someone else, and I felt relieved that his attention would be directed elsewhere. For the most part, it was, but he still managed to find time to harass me. I would be working behind the bar, engaging with patrons, when I would notice a red dot on my shirt: a light. Puzzled, I looked around to find its source, only to see Zack standing across the street, wielding a laser pointer. At thirty-two years old, this was the level to which he stooped to handle things. He continued to harass me for nearly two years, despite our short four-month situationship.

When he and his new girlfriend broke up, she reached out to me for help getting a restraining order. We exchanged brief accounts of our experiences, and I cautioned her about the things he'd put me through that she hadn't experienced yet.

Even though this woman chimed in with him in calling me a narcissist and all, I knew she was only hearing one side of the story and would eventually discover how he really was the hard way.

Did I help her?

No.

I was wary of getting involved and becoming a target of his again. I wished her well and hoped for the best for her. It turned out she didn't need my help anyway. She was capable of obtaining a restraining order all on her own. There are no hard feelings between the two of us, as we were both caught in the same situation and both had to learn how to deal with the aftermath of it all. She's now happily married to her own knight in shining armor, and I couldn't be happier for her.

Chapter 44

While I was bartending, one of my regulars brought in a friend of theirs—Joel, a guy I'd gone to high school with and had a brief encounter with years ago, but the timing wasn't quite right back then. They sat at the bar, placing their motorcycle helmets next to them, and we struck up a conversation. We reminisced about old times, sharing laughter and memories. He was still just as cute as ever and before he left, I invited him to stop in and see me any time.

A few weeks later, I learned that he'd been involved in a motorcycle accident. Wanting to offer our support, my coworker Tara and I decided to bake him some cookies and pay him a visit on one of our days off. We drove separately and, upon arriving at his place, the three of us sat in his living room. Joel recounted the story of what had led to his accident, while sitting in a rocking chair with his arm in a cast and road rash covering his leg, eating the cookies we brought him.

Tara had to head out, and I was going to follow suit when he asked if he could talk to me privately. Uncertain of what he wanted to discuss, I sat back down on the couch. That's when he asked if he could take me on a date—not immediately, but once he got well enough to do so. A proper date. Of course, I agreed. I gave him my phone number and told him to call me when he was ready; I would be waiting.

The apartment I'd recently moved into ended up flooding that February, leaving me with the daunting task of finding a new place to live within a mere two weeks. Balancing two jobs, ongoing classes, and now this unforeseen predicament proved to be quite overwhelming. Fortunately, I managed to secure another apartment, albeit in a lower-income complex, but it was decent enough. We moved in and did our best to get things back to normal.

I began to date Joel, and our relationship blossomed beautifully. We shared a strong connection, getting along effortlessly. His passion for outdoor adventures matched mine, and his laid-back demeanor meant we never found ourselves in arguments. He seamlessly integrated into my family and circle of friends.

I thought, *This could be it!*

Chapter 45

I'd applied for the dental hygiene program after finishing my prerequisites and was anxiously awaiting to see if I'd made the cut. The day arrived where that fateful letter holding my future came in the mail. Seated alone in my room, I closed the door and carefully tore open the envelope. With a mix of excitement and apprehension, I unfolded the piece of paper, preparing myself for the news it held.

I'd been accepted into the program.

I got in!

But the excitement didn't last as my mind quickly went to the financial aspect. I grabbed a notebook and a calculator and began calculating all of my expenses: tuition, books, and the balancing act between available work hours and essential bills. I entered the worst-case scenario figures, performing a few calculations and jotting down some notes. The final number I arrived at was far from reassuring. In light of this, I made the decision to reach out to the program director via email, seeking clarification on whether I would be able to maintain full-time employment while pursuing the program.

Her response confirmed my worst fears and dashed my hopes of escaping the bar scene to pursue a meaningful career—

one that Olivia could admire and be proud of. As I read her words, *"... students are unable to work full time due to the hours required to be in the clinic and the classroom,"* I could feel my bubble of hope burst. Was I condemned to a lifetime of being just a bartender? I'd proven that I could do so much more, but now that I was living on my own, it was so much harder.

Just as I was letting this information sink in, Joel walked in and caught me in my weak moment. In a moment of raw honesty, I allowed myself to break down in front of him, explaining that despite getting accepted into the program I'd worked tirelessly to qualify for, I wouldn't be able to pursue it. The financial constraints made it impossible for me.

I guess he'd been tossing around the idea of us moving in together because he asked me if we got a place together, did I think I could make it work? Given my past experiences, I was skeptical of moving in with another guy but in this situation, I saw it as a necessity. I could definitely pull this off with the burden of bills halved. He told me he loved me, and we would figure it all out together.

Wait a minute.

Did he just tell me he loved me?

He sure did.

We moved into a nice duplex just behind Olivia's school and not far from both of the jobs I worked. Olivia made friends with the neighbor behind us, and life was going good. The director of my program was nice enough to work with me on condensing my clinic days since I drove so far, allowing me to work at the dental office on the days I wasn't in class. I still worked at the bar on weekends and was able to save up a little bit of money; not much, but it was a small cushion, better than nothing.

My studies brought me a sense of fulfillment and intellectual stimulation. But whenever I tried to share my excitement about it with Joel, his dismissive response dampened my spirits. He often brushed off any conversation that required deeper thought, labeling himself as a "simple-minded plumber." This lack of intellectual engagement became a significant turn-off for me. I craved the idea of conversing with a partner who could match my intellectual curiosity, because to me, nothing is sexier than a man I can talk to.

* * *

Rain had fallen and the temperature had dropped, causing me to roll my SUV on the way home from class one evening. I found myself upright in the middle of a cornfield, my five-day-old coffee splattered across the SUV's interior, but miraculously, not a drop had landed on me. Gripping the wheel, I took a moment to process the events that had just unfolded. Fortunately, a truck waiting at the stoplight witnessed the entire incident and quickly came to my aid.

Once I shook off the initial shock, I called Joel to let him know what had happened, but I didn't anticipate the reaction I received.

"Great, how much is this gonna cost?" he grumbled.

There was no inquiry about whether I was hurt or needed a ride home—no offer of help or signs of concern for my well-being. His first thought was about the cost of fixing my SUV. Thanks to the sturdy craftsmanship of older vehicles, I was able to drive away with only cosmetic damage. It took a near-death experience for me to realize that perhaps Joel didn't care about me as much as I had hoped. This thought enveloped me in resignation.

Not again, I thought to myself.

Chapter 46

I was nearing the end of my hygiene school career, and the national and state boards were looming in my near future. Wanting to enjoy my upcoming spring break without the burden of studying, I made the decision to tackle my Local Anesthesia Board exam beforehand. I spent countless hours going over notes, watching videos, talking to people who had already taken the board, just trying to get a feel for what to study out of the endless information.

This was one of the most stressful times in my life. Failure was simply not an option for me—I couldn't afford the luxury of retaking any of the four exams. Consequently, I placed immense pressure on myself, a tendency I'd carried since childhood. The weight of this pressure resulted in countless sleepless nights spent scrolling through my phone until exhaustion finally overtook me.

It was the day before I took my Local Anesthesia Board exam, and a busy day at the dental office. I'd left my phone in the front office to charge while I was in the back assisting the dentist. When I finally had a moment to check my phone in the mid-afternoon, I was met with a flood of notifications: twelve missed calls and over twenty texts from Joel. Concerned that there might be an emergency, I quickly skimmed through the messages to grasp the situation before calling him back.

There was no emergency.

I scrolled through all his messages, filled with accusations, alleging that I was cheating and flirting with people on social media late into the night after he went to sleep. I was dumbfounded. Sure, I did stay up late on my phone sometimes, but it was because I was stressed, not because I was cheating! I let my thumbs get to work trying to explain how school had been overwhelming me and causing me to lose sleep.

Prove it.

Prove it, he texted back.

Really? How?

How was I supposed to prove that I was up all night scrolling on the internet saving recipes I would probably never cook? How was I supposed to prove that I was reviewing my online notes? He couldn't possibly be serious.

I decided to leave work and head home. Texting wasn't going to resolve anything; we needed to have a face-to-face conversation, one that a simple-minded plumber couldn't get out of. I pulled up in the drive and his car wasn't there. Figuring he hadn't returned from work yet, I entered the house, only to discover he had indeed been home—and had left me an unexpected surprise.

I was greeted with the sight of overturned plants and dirt strewn across the floor and in the carpet. Heading upstairs, I found my mattress haphazardly tossed atop the dresser, with the bed frame nowhere in sight. Anger surged within me. One of my biggest pet peeves is when people jump to conclusions without considering any other possibilities. He'd simply assumed that I'd done something without even considering anything else. I gave myself a minute to calm down. I walked back downstairs and grabbed a glass out of the cabinet. I poured myself a generous serving of vodka over ice and took a sip, allowing the cool liquid to soothe my frayed nerves.

I went back upstairs and started to clean up, placing my mattress on the floor and fixing the sheets. I carefully restored the plants to their upright positions and went to grab the vacuum out of the closet only to find it missing. That fucker made this mess and took the damn vacuum. Deep breaths…

I slipped on my shoes, vodka in hand, and headed to Walmart. I walked in there, drink and all, threw the cheapest vacuum they had in my cart, and headed to the checkout lane. If he thought he was going to let what he did phase me, he was sorely mistaken.

I got home and put my new vacuum to work, cleaning up the mess until everything was back in its rightful place, thankful that Olivia had gone over to a friend's house after school for a sleep over. But I wasn't done. After all the shit I'd been through, I wasn't about to go through it again. The night was young, and I was just getting started.

I began packing up all of Joel's belongings, moving them toward the front door. His kitchen table, dishes, clothes— everything was gathered and neatly arranged, waiting to be loaded up and taken away. The minute you opened the front door, it was all there, ready to go. I spent my entire night listening to music, drinking vodka, erasing any trace of him.

Midway through packing his belongings, he ended up texting me.

I'm sorry, I'll bring the bed frame back tomorrow.

I paused to take a break and glanced down at my phone. The

vodka had me feeling a little buzzed and without hesitation, I responded since I didn't need to think twice about my answer.

Don't bother, bring a truck instead. Your stuff is at the front door and ready to go.

It wasn't that I didn't care about him; I simply cared about myself more. Over time, I'd developed what I considered my superpower: the ability to cut someone off with a snap of my fingers and act as though they never existed. Later, my therapist would explain that this was a defense mechanism. But at that moment, it was what I needed to do to keep from completely falling apart.

Showered and dressed in my pajamas, I lay in bed, which was now nestled on the floor. With a notepad and calculator in hand, I found myself yet again faced with the task of rebuilding my life. Now that I only had myself to rely on financially, I needed to devise a plan for making it through the final two months of school. It was going to be a stretch, and it meant draining everything I'd saved, but I could do it… leaving me with $100 left over by the time I graduated.

Anyone else may have waved a white flag and given up. But for me, it fueled my motivation. With Olivia now older and capable of being at home alone, I took on additional jobs—first three, then four. When I wasn't in class, I was working tirelessly. And now that I was single again, I seized any opportunity to go out whenever I could, even if I only had $5 to spend.

That's when I met Kyle.

Chapter 47

Take a wild guess where I met this one.

No, for once we didn't have the high school connection, but you're right—we met at the bar. Kyle was like a lost puppy. His ex-wife had up and left him without warning. He came home one day and poof! She was gone. He was still piecing himself together from the wreckage she'd left behind, resorting to what I'd often found worked for me: self-medicating with alcohol. You think I would have learned my lesson by now, but there was that voice in my head saying, *"Here puppy, puppy, don't be scared, I'll take care of you."*

Idiot.

About two months into our relationship, I discovered he had another girl on the side. He was at a work function when I received a text from her, providing me with screenshots of their text conversations as evidence of their relationship. My initial reaction? Finally, a girl who is a girl's girl. Though I knew I had no right to be angry with her, I couldn't help but feel a twinge of hatred. However, that dissipated quickly as my anger shifted toward the scumbag who was cheating on me. I forwarded the screen shots she'd sent to me to him.

My phone started blowing up with calls and texts from him.

I'm so sorry.

Please answer, I can explain.

Despite my anger, I still couldn't shake the sympathy I felt for him. I understood the confusion that follows a divorce all too well. It's a whirlwind of anxiety and uncertainty. With that in mind, I made the decision to give him one more chance. But I made it clear: if he fucked up again, it would be the end of us.

He wasn't a bad person, and despite being cap-fished, I chose to overlook it. Yes, cap-fished—when a guy consistently wears a ball cap or hat they look good in, but when they take it off, they're bald as a baby. I also tried to ignore the fact that he had the palate of an eight-year-old and was a functioning alcoholic. But beyond that, he had a lively group of friends, and I genuinely enjoyed the social aspect of our budding relationship.

I made efforts to encourage him to eat more home-cooked meals by bringing over groceries and preparing dinners to enjoy at his place. His habit of sleeping on the floor was something I wasn't particularly fond of. Whenever I stayed over, I tried to persuade him to sleep in his bed instead of the floor that his dog had pissed all over.

He had a decent house but instead of investing in it, he spent his money on alcohol and gambling. Basic necessities like a functioning dryer were neglected, leaving his clothes smelling musty. He didn't even own a winter coat, so for Christmas, I bought him one so he wouldn't freeze to death. As time went on, I started to feel more like his mother than his girlfriend. I couldn't comprehend how a grown man could willingly neglect to take care of himself or his home.

He gave me permission to redo his kitchen one weekend while he was out of town. I took on the challenge eagerly, repainting the walls, installing a stylish backsplash, and resurfacing the countertops. Sure, I may have fucked the countertops up for any future sale of the house, but it was a vast improvement over what he had before. I couldn't wait for him—and his friends—to see the transformation, and I was happy that they all seemed amazed at what I'd completed in such a short amount of time. Even though he was happy with how it turned out, deep down I think he felt slightly demasculated.

He became upset with me one day when I insisted on going to the hardware store to get a new cord for the broken dryer. Unfortunately, we ended up getting the wrong one, so we called it a night without fixing it. Later, during a group text with our friends, I mentioned what we'd attempted to do and he took offense, feeling as though I was portraying him as incapable of doing anything. This, of course, made me upset in return. I got up, put on my shoes, and walked out the door.

All I was trying to do was help him, and he couldn't see that. It didn't take me mentioning our attempt to fix his broken dryer for anyone to realize his struggles with basic tasks. They already knew. I felt like I was pouring my energy into a lost cause. He was content sleeping on piss-soaked carpet, eating chicken tenders and french fries, and drowning himself in alcohol until the day he died. I knew my efforts were being wasted, but I didn't want to add another failed relationship to my growing list. I kept on trying.

Chapter 48

Kyle had gone out of town for a basketball tournament with his dad and brother for the weekend, and I'd come down with the flu, forcing me to call off work that Friday. As Saturday rolled around, Bryan's brother Justin unexpectedly texted me.

Hey, what are you doing tonight? I have my work Christmas party and my date ditched me. Wanna go? Free steak dinner?

Feeling significantly better and quite hungry, plus considering it was Justin, I replied, asking what time I should be ready.

I got dressed and ready to go, texting Kyle that I was going to go with Justin to this party, not expecting the response I got in return. He was pissed, as if I was expected to stay home sick all weekend. I knew he was drunk, as usual, but his behavior still caught me off guard. I assured him I felt much better and reminded him that Justin was like a brother to me, trying to ease his concerns. With that being said, I left it at that and headed out for the night.

The Christmas party turned out to be enjoyable; I spent most of the time chatting with Kerri, Bryan and Justin's younger sister, whom I'd set up with one of Justin's co-workers. While we sat at our table, enjoying our cocktails, I received a text from Kyle.

WE ARE DONE.

We are done?

All caps. He meant business.

I turned my phone to Kerri to share what Kyle had sent and proceeded to explain why he was upset with me. One of the things I appreciated about Kerri was her straightforwardness—she didn't hesitate to speak her mind. She clinked her glass with mine.

"Good riddance. You can do so much better."

She was right.

And there were those words my sister had told me back when I got divorced: never settle.

The rest of the night was a blast. After leaving the party, we headed to a different bar where we danced until the early hours. It felt great to spend time with them, even though we weren't technically family. For Olivia's sake, I'd always considered them family. We were all just kids when I had Olivia, and it was a challenging situation for everyone involved.

The next morning, I received a text from Kyle, apologizing and claiming he was just kidding. But the truth was, I wasn't kidding. I wasn't sixteen anymore. I didn't engage in that back-and-forth, break-up-and-get-back-together drama. I knew what I wanted from a relationship, and I knew I wouldn't find it with him. It was over. He could go back to whoever that girl was when we first started dating. And just like that, my superpower kicked in.

With Joel and Kyle, I realized that I'd inadvertently imposed a two-year time frame on our relationship. If things weren't evolving as I'd hoped or if something occurred that made me doubt our future together, I tended to call it quits rather than fight to salvage the relationship. Having already invested so much time in undeserving partners, I was unwilling to find myself in another situation where my time and efforts were wasted.

I stayed single for a bit, focusing on myself and Olivia. I was making better money as a dental hygienist working just as much as I had before. I slowly began to put myself out there, dabbling in the dating apps. It was a mixed experience at best—swiping left, swiping right. To my dismay, many of the people I came across were familiar faces, leading to frustration and ultimately prompting me to delete the app.

I received the occasional message in my social media inbox. While I entertained some, others quickly crossed boundaries, prompting me to block them after receiving inappropriate messages. I was tired of being objectified. I wasn't out to date for the sake of dating. My intentions weren't casual. I was seeking something serious. If that wasn't what they were looking for, then they could leave me the fuck alone.

Chapter 49

When loneliness crept in, I would go on dates, genuinely attempting to forge a connection with someone. And in some ways, I did—but it wasn't the deep connection I was truly seeking. What I yearned for was someone who met all my criteria: good looking, took care of himself, stable, and family-oriented. I didn't think those were unreasonable expectations, yet I was shocked by how challenging it was to find someone who checked all of the boxes.

I got a message one day from a guy named Leo on social media, trying to initiate small talk. I took the bait out of boredom. He had a decent sense of humor and, after some quick online sleuthing, I agreed to let him take me out to dinner.

He picked me up, even got out of his truck to open the door for me, a gesture I found impressive. He'd chosen a restaurant about half an hour away, giving us plenty of time to chat and get to know each other during the car ride. I'd grown so jaded from my past experiences and weary of wasting time that I didn't hesitate to get right to it.

In that thirty minutes, I laid it all out on the table. I

shared every awful thing I'd done and recounted much of the hardship I'd endured, including my divorce and past relationship struggles. I wrapped it up by stating that I wasn't interested in casual dating or messing around. I was seeking something serious and if that wasn't what he was looking for, he could turn the car around and take me home.

He continued driving to the restaurant, which led me to believe he was okay with all the information I'd just unloaded on him. He was older than me, and he expressed that he was seeking the same thing—a serious relationship. This gave me a glimmer of hope that perhaps I'd finally found someone who knew exactly what he wanted. For once.

He had two girls around the same age as Olivia, which was a bonus for me since I'd always wanted her to have siblings but never found the right person to give her any. As we continued to date, he would occasionally stop by my workplace and surprise me with a coffee since he was working just down the road. No one had ever shown me that kind of attention before, and I couldn't help but appreciate it.

He was in the process of moving and searching for a new house. With his own house sold, he had limited time to find a new home. He assured me that he fully intended for Olivia and me to move in with him and was actively seeking a home that could accommodate us all. I was both taken aback and excited by this prospect. However, I wasn't willing to leave our current home so easily. We'd been living in the duplex for five years now, the longest we'd stayed in one place. I wasn't keen on uprooting Olivia again unless it was something she agreed to and unless I was certain it would lead to marriage in the future.

I expressed my concerns to Leo about the situation. It was

encouraging to have someone listen to my thoughts and take them into consideration. He understood where I was coming from and reassured me that he wanted the same things I did. While I wanted to believe him, I couldn't help but keep my guard up, having been fooled so many times before.

Chapter 50

Leo found a house that could accommodate all of us. While I stood firm about not immediately moving in, I offered my assistance with the move and even volunteered to help with the renovations as the house needed some remodeling. After work, I would head to his new home, spending my evenings with him, tackling tasks like cutting tile, laying hardwood floors, and resurfacing cabinets, among others. I put a lot of effort into helping him transform the house, and I felt proud of what we accomplished together.

As we were getting ready to grout the backsplash to finish off the kitchen renovation, I couldn't help but notice his impatience. It was a trait that had become increasingly apparent throughout the entire process. His tendency to rush often led to mistakes and mishaps along the way.

He started smearing the grout onto the tiles before I had a chance to lay down a barrier on the new countertop. I managed to cover some areas with cloth before he reached them, but the spots I missed were already covered in white grout that had dropped. Despite my suggestion to cover the countertops, he didn't listen. The countertops were made of dark quartz and porous, and I was worried about the grout staining them.

He finished and began wiping up the grout, only to discover that the white had absorbed into the quartz, leaving it discolored. He flew into a fit of laughter, throwing things, screaming at the top of his lungs. I stood there silently, observing his outburst. I refused to be caught in the crossfire of his temper and I walked out. This was the first sign of his temper that he'd let slip. After he'd cooled down, he called me to apologize, but I was unsure whether to go back or not. In the end, I decided to go home and call it a night, especially since I had to work the next morning.

I reasoned with myself, reminding myself that people react differently when they're upset. Who was I to judge someone's reaction to stress? I wasn't excusing his behavior, or so I believed; I was simply trying to understand it. I didn't want to let one incident tarnish my opinion of him. I decided to attribute it to the stress he was under from remodeling his entire house and preparing it for his kids to move in. Perhaps it was just a one-time thing.

During this time, I underwent testing to see if I would be a match to donate one of my kidneys to my aunt, who was in need. Several family members were tested, but only one match was found: my mother. Unfortunately, her kidney function was too low to donate. I figured if she was a match, there was a good chance I would be too. After confirming that our blood types were compatible, I made numerous trips to the University of Chicago for labs, heart and lung scans, and injections of iodine that momentarily made my body feel like it was on fire. Each lab visit involved drawing about twenty-seven vials of blood, sometimes leaving me on the verge of passing out. I grew weary of being poked and prodded, wondering if they would ever determine if I was a match.

Finally, we received the news we'd hoped for, and we set a date for the donation as soon as possible.

I informed Leo about the surgery, and he appeared supportive. On the day of the procedure, I told him I would text him to update him on how everything went. I didn't want many visitors. I was only going to be in the hospital for a day, so it didn't seem necessary. He could come see me at my place once I returned home, if he wished.

The surgery went smoothly, although it was quite an experience. My entire body ached from being inflated like a balloon so the robot could perform its task. Due to the opioid epidemic, I was only prescribed basic over-the-counter pain medication that you could find at any local pharmacy. Needless to say, I was eager to return to the comforts of my own home.

Leo visited with his kids the day after I returned home. I was so exhausted that I only let him stay for a few minutes. He was irritated and didn't seem to grasp the toll the surgery had taken on my body, which was now working extra hard to regain its normal function. I wasn't up for much conversation and moving was difficult, except when necessary, like getting up to use the bathroom. I needed more time to recuperate before I could spend time with him like before.

After two weeks, I returned to work, taking things slow to avoid overdoing it. Leo had completed many of the small tasks around his house and wanted me to stop by to see the progress. I brought Olivia along so she could see what I'd been working on during the nights she was at her job. While the house looked better than when we'd started, it still needed some finishing touches. As I showed Olivia around, I asked her how she would feel about us moving there, explaining that Leo had invited us to be part of his household.

Chapter 51

I'd given serious thought to this decision. The idea of living in a spacious house was appealing, but I wasn't going to let that be the sole factor. Olivia's well-being and comfort were paramount. She was a teenager now, and I wanted her to have a say in our future. If she wasn't on board or didn't feel comfortable with it, then the idea would be off the table. I knew she had her own concerns, considering it wasn't the first time I'd made a significant life change, and the instances of rebuilding our lives were adding up. However, Leo was the first person who genuinely seemed like a family man, someone who prioritized his children and wanted to include us in his life. Olivia would have a room twice as big as her current one and her own bathroom. While she was excited about the idea, I encouraged her to take her time and think it over carefully.

After careful consideration, we left our home of five years and moved in with Leo. I spent a lot of time turning the house into a home, decorating and buying furniture, adding the finishing touches that it needed. It took time, but after two years, things were finally starting to come together.

I found myself spending most of my evenings and weekends

cleaning up after everyone. Before I moved in, Leo's mom used to come by and clean for him, but I didn't think it was necessary. Surely, it couldn't be that bad, right? I knew it would take some effort to break the habit of living in a mess, so I began asking for help with certain chores around the house. Fortunately, I never encountered any resistance when asking for assistance.

It became a lot to keep up with. I would spend hours cleaning, only for everything to be undone in a matter of minutes. I left notes, asking politely for simple tasks like putting dishes in the dishwasher, but they often went ignored. Wet towels would lie on the floor for days before I could address them, and clothing seemed to find its way into every corner of the house. No one bothered to let the dog out, resulting in accidents on the new carpet. I found myself renting a carpet cleaner once a month just to maintain the carpets, which were only a few months old.

Amid all of this, I started to notice the stark difference in their family dynamic. Their primary mode of communication seemed to be through fighting. This was something I found hard to absorb. Leo would engage in heated arguments with his kids like they were grown adults, and they would fight right back. I felt compelled to intervene and defend the kids, but I quickly realized that this was simply how they interacted. I learned that this was just what they did and decided that it was best for me to not get involved.

It was hard to sit there and listen to him yell obscenities at them. He would tell the oldest that she was a bitch, just like her mom. It was disheartening to see how far he would go during their arguments, and it made me worry about how he might treat me if we were to disagree. I made a firm decision that

I would only intervene if the situation escalated to physical violence.

I started to observe a pattern: he rarely had anything positive to say about anyone. Every comment that left his mouth seemed to carry a negative tone. He often ridiculed people for trivial matters, even things beyond their control, such as their appearance, manner of speech, marital status, choice of vehicle, haircut, or even the physical appearance of their children. The list could go on, but I think you understand the gist of it. His conversations were consistently steeped in negativity, and despite my attempts to inject some positivity or encourage a different perspective, he remained steadfast in his negative views.

Any time he had a drink in his hand, it was always a beer. He drank every day, but he worked hard every day too. I didn't mind him having a few drinks after work; it seemed like a well-deserved reward. However, over time, I began to notice a troubling pattern: his drinking seemed to exacerbate his already volatile temper. This, in turn, fueled arguments and created a tense atmosphere where everyone felt like they had to tread carefully around him.

He wasn't like this all the time; we did have enjoyable moments and shared fun times together. I liked attending family gatherings and his kids' sports games, and he accompanied me to some of my own family events, although his interaction there was minimal. I found myself gradually spending less time with my own family to avoid any discomfort or awkwardness that arose from having him around them.

Our relationship lacked many things, with one of the primary ones being affection. There were moments when it felt like we were simply roommates. When we went to bed, he would often turn away and fall asleep without any form of physical affection. There were no kisses, hugs, or any signs of caring displayed toward me. The only time he showed any affection was when he felt someone else was looking at me, or if he perceived that I was showing interest in someone else.

Yet he expected me to be a porn star in the bedroom. This became a constant source of complaint from him—that I never wanted to be intimate with him. I'm sorry, but it's hard to want to do that with someone who is constantly in a sour mood. I would try to explain that my reluctance wasn't due to a lack of desire, but rather a need for attention and affection from him. I couldn't simply fulfill his desires whenever he demanded it; I didn't work that way. As much as I tried to explain, he didn't care. In his eyes, the issue was with me, not with him, and I was the one who needed to change.

Was I really destined to live such a loveless life? I wasn't asking for much, just a little affection every now and then, perhaps some acknowledgment born from positivity instead of jealousy. Yet my pleas went unanswered. I begged, even cried, for simple gestures like holding my hand or sitting with me on the couch. These were requests he couldn't seem to honor, yet he could spend a solid twenty minutes saying goodnight to his dog, showering her with kisses and attention—the very attention I craved. I felt so neglected in that aspect of my life that I was jealous of a fucking dog.

Chapter 52

Olivia invited friends over to film a class project. I was lying in bed, in a bout of depression caused by a recent argument with Leo. He was mad about an innocent exchange between a male friend of mine and me on my social media page that he took as flirtatious, accusing me of seeking attention from other men. And I'll admit, maybe subconsciously I was. I wasn't getting any attention from him at home unless it came in the form of a negative comment. When someone had something nice to say to me, I ate it up.

When I heard him walk in the house, I turned on my side, facing away from the closed bedroom door, hoping he would think I was sleeping and leave me alone when he entered. He walked in, creating a racket with no regard for whether I was sleeping or not. In my effort to avoid a conversation, I rose and headed to the bathroom, ignoring his presence as I passed by. Yet he insisted on talking. My repeated refusals didn't deter him. Instead, he began to do what he did best: poke the bear.

I stood at the sink as I endured his onslaught of criticism. He tore into me about things from my past, throwing each word like a dagger at my back. He dredged up moments from my married life, a period when he wasn't even present yet felt entitled to pass judgment on. Accusations of fabricated scenarios flew, his attempts to rationalize my behavior to fit his narrative.

Who in the hell did he think he was? The same guy who got pissed at me for calling him an asshole when he was undeniably being an asshole. And now he was attacking me with things I'd confided in him, personal information that I trusted him with, thinking he was a mature adult. He weaponized my vulnerabilities to tear down my defenses. My hands gripped the edge of the sink as the sound of his voice hammered away.

"Stop it. Please. Stop."

I struggled to maintain my composure, pleading with him to leave me be, but he persisted, leaving the room only to return and resume his tirade. I finally hit my breaking point.

As he reentered the bathroom, finding me still standing there, hands clenched around the sink, he resumed his relentless barrage about my past. That's when I snapped. Without a second thought, I grabbed the vase from the sink, raised it high, and brought it crashing down, shattering it into countless pieces on the floor.

"*Shut the fuckkkkk upppppppppppp!*"

I unleashed all that I'd let build up inside me over the past year and a half, telling him I was leaving, and even stooping to his level by suggesting it was no wonder why his ex had left him. All while he acted unaware of his role in provoking my outburst. He'd purposely pushed me beyond my limits and now he stood there, laughing and mocking me. In my blind rage, I forgot that Olivia had friends over; they'd all borne witness to the unfolding scene.

I entered the kitchen to find it empty, realizing that Olivia and her friends, who had been filming there, were gone. Of all the moments for him to stir up trouble, it had to be now. Ignoring his shouts from behind me reminding me that I had nowhere else to go, I grabbed my purse to leave. He may have been right about my lack of options, but it didn't mean I had to stay there.

I was fortunate to have a good relationship with my boss back then. He allowed me to spend the night at the office, even bringing over a six-pack of Coors Lite, knowing I was upset. I settled into one of the dental chairs after getting word from Olivia that she wasn't coming home, sipping a beer and ignoring Leo's calls as I gradually drifted off to sleep.

The next day, I reluctantly answered his call and accepted his apology with only partial sincerity. What choice did I have? He was right; I had nowhere else to go, and spending every night at work wasn't a sustainable solution. I had to swallow my pride and return, hoping things would improve. Alternatively, I needed to actively work on improving the situation until I was able to find a place of my own.

Olivia's anger was justified, and I knew it. I'd inadvertently embarrassed her in front of her friends, and try as I might, I couldn't find the right words to explain the situation to her. Even if I could, I doubted it would have made things any better. The weight of that remorse weighed heavily on me then, and it still does to this day. This incident strained our relationship, and no matter how much I apologized, I couldn't fully mend the damage it had caused.

How could I expect her to know or understand everything I was dealing with, when I never said a word about it? I had a hard enough time trying to explain away the constant yelling and fighting between Leo and his kids. Our household had become a war zone, with potential conflicts lurking around every corner. I masked my reality with a smile, burying myself in work and household chores to evade any discussion about it.

When I realized that when she said she wasn't coming home it was a permanent statement, and she'd made the decision to move in with a friend. It felt like my world crumbled around me. Anger welled up inside me. But as I reflected on it, I realized that most of that anger was directed inward, at myself, more than anyone else.

Chapter 53

The dishwasher hummed in the background, and I'd just finished tidying up the pots and pans from preparing Christmas dinner for everyone. Leo and his kids were glued to the TV. It was around 8:00 p.m., and finally, I could change into something cozy, settle down, and unwind after a long day of hosting his family. Just as I sank into the chair, ready to relax, my phone lit up with the name "Dad" on the screen.

Shit.

I forgot to call my dad to say merry Christmas.

I rose from my seat and made my way down the hallway before answering, greeting him warmly and mentioning that I was just about to call him myself.

"Is this Holly Wells?"

I stopped in my tracks. "Dad, it's Holly."

Something was wrong.

"This is the Porter County Sheriff's Department. Is this Holly Wells?"

My heart began to pound, beating faster, causing my ears to burn.

"Yes, this is Holly."

"We regret to inform you that your father has passed away in his home."

"Shut the fuck up!"

As I dropped the phone, Leo's gaze shifted toward me, prompting me to hastily retrieve it to catch the rest of the conversation. Perched on the edge of the bed, I listened intently as they filled me in. It turned out that my stepmom had provided them with my phone number and instructed them to reach out to me. When I inquired about what had happened, they explained that it seemed to be from natural causes and that he'd passed away peacefully. With each detail, my heart broke a little more.

I hurriedly changed out of my pajamas, grabbing whatever clothes I could reach and throwing them on. As I did, Leo entered the room and asked what was happening.

"My dad…. He's… dead."

My dad was dead. The words felt surreal as they left my lips. Ignoring his presence, I pushed past him and rushed to my car, desperate to get to my dad's house. The weight of the upcoming phone calls to my sisters loomed over me like a dark cloud.

As I pulled up to the house, I noticed the coroner's vehicle parked in the driveway, alongside a police car. With a sense of urgency, I sprinted into the house, where I found my stepbrother already present, and my stepmom engaged in conversation with an officer.

"Where is he?"

My stepmom approached me, her lips dry and cracked from dehydration, but my focus was solely on seeing my dad. They led me to his room, where he lay in his bed, lifeless. The reality of the situation hit me like a ton of bricks.

I sat beside him, taking his stiff hand in mine, tears streaming down my face as I gazed at his peaceful yet empty-eyed expression. As I held onto him, my stepmom hovered nearby, rambling on about my dad's obesity and how this wasn't the man she'd married. Despite her words, I did my best to block her out, focusing instead on reliving the precious moments I'd had with my father.

The coroner called me into the kitchen, where he proceeded to inquire about my dad's health and any potential issues that could be related to his sudden passing. I did my best to provide answers to his questions. Afterward, he handed me his business card and advised me to reach out if I had any further questions. Meanwhile, outside, they solemnly wheeled my dad's body out in a body bag on a gurney.

With my other stepbrother now present, he attended to my stepmom, who appeared delusional due to dehydration and lack of sustenance. She rambled on about my dad's weight and how she believed that to be the cause of his death, repeating sentiments she would express even in good health. However, I couldn't shake the suspicion that they might have COVID-19. And in my gut, I believed that was what ultimately led to my dad's passing.

As my stepbrother and I sat at the table, we began making a list of tasks that needed to be addressed. Meanwhile, my stepmom wasted no time in clearing out my dad's belongings from his closet and dresser. Despite her frailty, she managed to gather some of his things into bags for me to take home. My stepbrother was aware of where my dad kept a bottle of whiskey, something both of us felt we needed in that moment. We poured ourselves a shot, knocking it back before refilling our glasses.

Merry Christmas.

Chapter 54

In the aftermath of my dad's passing, I hoped for some semblance of support from Leo, especially considering I'd been there to console him when his dad passed away. However, all I received was a brief hug and an "I'm sorry." I suppose there's really nothing anyone can do to alleviate the pain of such a loss, so his actions or lack thereof ultimately didn't matter. Still, I wished for the same level of empathy that I'd extended to him during his own time of grief, and it was disheartening not to receive it.

The loss of my dad, coupled with the recent passing of another one of my relatives and the ongoing challenges with Olivia and my family, became unbearable. I sought out help from a therapist and unloaded everything I was going through. He was able to provide me with invaluable emotional support during some of my darkest moments. For years, I'd grappled with feelings of self-doubt and questioning my sanity, but as my therapist carefully unraveled the complexities of my experiences, he helped me realize that my actions were grounded in valid reasons. He illuminated how the circumstances I faced compelled me to take action and survive the best way I knew how. I'd lived in survival mode for so long,

I knew no other way. Finally, I felt truly listened to, and for the first time in a long while, I regained a sense of control over my life.

Going to therapy was the mental investment I never knew I needed. I was surrounded with negativity and it was taking a toll on me mentally, emotionally, and physically. I had to decide what kind of life I wanted to live, not what kind of life someone else wanted me to have. I had to break this cycle of poor relationships that I constantly found myself in no matter how uncomfortable it made me. I had to face my emotions as they presented themselves instead of suppressing them until I exploded. I had to dig up what was buried internally in order to save myself at the time and own it all. And I would begin with my daughter.

Olivia had moved on to college. She allowed me to assist her in finding an apartment and getting settled in, and I did my utmost to support her transition into adulthood. Before I departed, I ensured she was well prepared by stocking her pantry with groceries and preparing meals for her. Although I was taking steps to mend our relationship, I knew things wouldn't get better unless I allowed myself to step out of my comfort zone.

Leo's daughter had a soccer game not far from Olivia's apartment, so I borrowed his truck and drove over. I'd told her I wanted to talk to her briefly, assuring her I wouldn't take up too much of her time. I firmly believed that change starts with one person, and that person had to be me. Sitting on the edge of her bed in her studio apartment, I gathered the courage I needed to speak my truth, and finally, I let it all out.

After years of being strong and living in survival mode, I finally allowed myself to be vulnerable in her presence. Tears flowed freely as I laid bare my emotions. I needed her to see that underneath my hard exterior, I was just as human as anyone else.

I wanted to be her mom, and I hoped for her acceptance. It was the maternal connection I lacked with my own mother that I sought with her. Expressing my love was crucial, as those words were scarce in my upbringing, and I understood the loneliness it breeds. We agreed on weekly calls, and I pledged to thaw the icy exterior I'd developed. It would take time, but I was willing to do whatever I needed to do to regain my daughter's trust and have her back in my life.

I left there with a new outlook on life. The steps I was taking to better my mental health were paying off in big ways. I knew I was on the right track, and I needed to trust my instincts when it came to how I dealt with the next task on my list.

I needed to figure out a way to deal with Leo and his negative ass.

Chapter 55

One of my patients at work turned out to be a classmate from high school. While we weren't close back then, reconnecting as patient and healthcare provider sparked conversations about people we both knew. He mentioned working in insurance and offered to provide me with a quote if I was considering a switch. Since I'd stuck with the same insurance provider since I started driving, I thought it might be worth exploring other options. We exchanged numbers, and he assured me he would reach out soon.

I swung by his office one evening after work to finalize paperwork for my new insurance. Conveniently, his office was adjacent to a bar, and we decided to grab a beer after I'd signed everything. As we reminisced about our younger days, laughing at the foolishness of our youth, it struck us as amusing that our paths had never crossed until now. After settling our tab, I found myself not quite ready to head home. It was Friday night, and I was in high spirits. I suggested we hit up another local bar for another round, and I phoned Leo to join us.

I dialed Leo as we headed to the bar, asking if he wanted to meet us at the bar near our house. I filled him in on the details of my friend, exactly who he was and why I was with him, although he was already aware. Leo confirmed he would join us, so we snagged three seats at the bar and ordered drinks and food. Our conversation flowed, laughing about our high school escapades, all the while keeping an eye on the door for Leo's arrival so I could flag him down.

Our food arrived and our conversation naturally quieted down as we ate, but after two bites, we were interrupted by Leo. I must have missed him entering the bar and taking a seat across the way. He'd sat there watching my every move like a psychopath. He charged toward us, throwing accusations of flirting and cheating at me. My appetite vanished as embarrassment swallowed me whole. He was making a scene in front of everyone, people I knew. I ineffectively kept trying to get him to calm down. It seemed any innocent socializing triggered his temper and jealousy. I guess I wasn't allowed to do that with anyone.

The owner of the bar, also someone I knew, witnessed what had happened and approached to manage the scene. I boxed my food and settled the tab for both my friend and myself, apologizing for putting him in this situation. I made sure my friend left before I did, to ensure that Leo didn't follow him out into the parking lot. Just before I left, I confronted Leo directly and looked him dead in the eye.

"Why in the *fuck* would I invite you here if I was up to no good? He's married with a kid and baby on the way. What in the *fuck* is wrong with you?"

Just then, the owner pulled me aside and asked if I was okay.

"It would be in your best interest if you got this guy out of your bar as quickly as possible, but I would appreciate it if you made sure I was out of the parking lot before you did."

He got the message and intervened, restraining Leo while I made my exit. I held back my tears until I walked through the door. Once I got in my car, fear set in.

I sped home, ignoring all the calls and texts pouring in from Leo, frantically packing a bag in hopes of leaving before he arrived. I stuffed essentials into a backpack—makeup, toothbrush, phone charger—grabbed a few beers from the fridge, and raced out of the driveway with no particular destination in mind. I knew I couldn't be there when he got home. The look in his eyes at the bar was chilling; he only saw what he wanted to see, refusing to acknowledge the truth. It was pointless to argue with him when he always believed he was right.

I texted my friend to make sure he'd arrived home safely and to apologize once more for the night's chaos. I sensed his sympathy and embarrassment on my behalf. He asked if I was okay and if I needed anything.

A place to stay for the night.

We stayed up most of the night sharing beers while he listened to me open up about my relationship with Leo. I tried to make light of it at times, and he made an effort to lift my spirits, which I appreciated, because crying in front of people wasn't something I was used to doing.

Chapter 56

Carly arranged a hotel room for me for the next night; not that I couldn't afford it, but because she knew that I wouldn't spend the money on it. She worried I would end up going back to the house, where I would feel forced to reconcile. I waited until I knew Leo would be gone so I could go pick up my cat and found a way to smuggle her into the hotel room without being noticed.

I took a shower and made myself as comfortable as I could before sitting in bed attempting to unwind. Instead of finding peace, I found myself wrestling with a difficult decision: return to a loveless relationship or embark on the journey of rebuilding my life once again? As I pondered, my thoughts turned to my dad.

Dad had been waiting for the day my stepmom died so he could return to Tennessee and be happy, and now that would never happen. As much as I loved my dad, I didn't want to end up like him, just waiting for the other person to die so I could be happy. I didn't want to be stuck in a relationship where I was begging for attention and affection, as I'd been doing. I knew I deserved better. In my determination to avoid another failed relationship, I found myself going against my sister's advice and settling for the situation I was in, making excuses for it along the way.

That wasn't the life I wanted for myself.

The next day, I called around, looking for a storage unit, and lucked out when I secured the last larger unit at the place just down the road from the house. I didn't want Leo there when I moved my things out, so I told him that I would come by while he was at work and get it all out then. There really wasn't much to argue about, but of course he found something.

He wanted to know every detail: where I was going, who was helping me. Where I was moving to was none of his business. To me, it didn't matter who was helping me move, as long as I got my things out of there, right?

Wrong.

Since it was *his* house, I wasn't "allowed" to have anyone of the male species set foot on his property. As ridiculous as his demand was, I agreed to it and enlisted one of my girlfriends— Christy— and her mom. My days of feeding his need for confrontation were done.

We arrived early and spent hours packing and loading my life into the U-Haul I'd rented. I wasn't concerned with how things were loaded up, as long as I got it into the truck. I could always organize it later. Christy and I worked tirelessly, getting everything packed up quicker than we thought. As we loaded up the last of the boxes, Leo's mom and aunt pulled up to the house.

I knew he hadn't told them what was going on, so it fell upon me to deliver the news. Seeing them approach with tears already welling up, I wrapped my arms around them and hugged them tight. I told them I couldn't continue with his behavior anymore. Leo needed help, and not the kind that

I could provide. As sad as they were that I was leaving, they understood how he was, and they weren't entirely surprised that I'd reached my limit with him.

Even as I was leaving, my thoughts weren't solely centered on myself. I chose to leave behind my couches, kitchen table, patio furniture, and even my Christmas tree—not for his sake, but for his children's comfort. As I did one last walk through to make sure I hadn't overlooked anything, I took in the state of the house. This may have been his house, but I was the one who gave it warmth. I was the one who made it a home. Now, it was nothing more than a hollow shell of its former self. I bid farewell to the countless hours of effort and emotion I'd invested, walking away and leaving it all behind.

I felt hopeful as I settled in at my aunt Brenda and uncle Tom's house. Although I'd vowed to never talk to Leo again, I'd forgotten to get my things that were stored in the attic. I was forced to contact him about it, and he offered to help me bring them to my storage unit. I knew he would find a way to somehow use that against me, claiming that I'd taken advantage of him or something along those lines. I didn't want his help, but I reluctantly agreed. The sooner I could get this done, the better.

He followed me to my storage unit and helped me unload everything. I cleared out his truck first, hoping he would leave shortly after. I thanked him for his help and dismissed him, but he wouldn't leave.

"This is how you're going to treat me after I just helped you?"

Ah, there it was.

The help that I'd refused but he'd insisted on. Now, when he went and told everyone what happened, he could make me out to be the asshole.

He stood there watching me as I rearranged boxes to accommodate the items I'd just unloaded. He continued to tell me that he didn't want any of this, that the situation was entirely my fault. Over and over and over. Each time he spoke, I reiterated my request for him to leave.

I found myself transported back to that moment in the bathroom, where his relentless prodding had eventually pushed me to my breaking point. Throwing words like daggers at me, aimed to pierce and provoke until I broke down and gave him what he wanted. Well, I wasn't going to give him the satisfaction. Not anymore.

He ignored my repeated requests for him to leave. Instead, he responded with pointing his finger at me once again, placing the blame on me. Frustrated beyond measure, I grabbed the nearest object, turned around, and hurled it at him with all the force I could muster.

"Get the fuck out of my life!"

I screamed with such ferocity that my ear drums felt like they'd ruptured from the sheer amount of force that it took. I couldn't have cared less if anyone overheard or what he thought of me. I just wanted him to go the fuck away forever. And after that, he did.

Chapter 57

I stayed with my aunt and uncle for a few months before moving in with a newly divorced friend of mine. Although the outcome of our friendship wasn't a lasting one like I'd hoped, the few months of staying there provided me with the space and independence I desperately needed. My time spent there was far from wasted, allowing me to hunker down and figure out what I truly wanted out of life.

I decided I didn't want to be in any kind of relationship for the foreseeable future. I made a conscious decision to prioritize my personal growth and independence over romantic entanglements, focusing on my career and enjoying quality time with my friends and traveling instead. It's unfortunate that some of my attempts to maintain male friendships didn't pan out as expected.

After a few months, I began to feel the weight of loneliness. I decided I would give the online dating world a go, and I signed up for nearly all of the free ones I could find. Swipe left, swipe right, ignore message after message… all of the usual suspects once again. I finally decided to sign up for a paid service, thinking that the variety and intentions of the men on there would be different. I quickly learned that this wasn't the case. After weeding through the familiar faces, I agreed to a few dates which all led to nothing, and not because of them. Because of me.

I'd set high standards. Was this my fault? Not necessarily. Given everything I'd been through, I didn't want to go through any of it again. Even though my standards were high, they weren't unreasonable. Take care of yourself—mentally and physically—don't be an alcoholic or drug addict, no anger issues, in touch with your emotions, stable, not jealous of male friends, not controlling, not a narcissist… I'm pretty sure you can see where I'm going with this. You would be surprised how hard this was to find.

I became strangely upset after a guy I went on a few dates with decided we would be better off as friends—mostly because I realized that maybe I was the problem. Maybe all of those idiots were right: something must be wrong with me since I continued to find myself in this endless loop of losers. I was coming to the harsh conclusion that maybe I was meant to be alone, and I should give up on finding my soul mate. As each day passed, I was becoming more accepting of living alone with a hundred cats.

I logged in and deactivated all my dating apps one by one. Delete. Delete. Delete. When I got to the last one, the fresh faces of my new matches appeared once I was logged in. One face in particular looked familiar. I decided to make one last ditch effort and sent a message to the familiar face containing my phone number and what I'd come to find to be my favorite pick-up line:

Hey, didn't we go to high school together?

I hit Send and deactivated my account shortly after.

It took a couple of days, but I finally got a message from him.

After a little back and forth, we agreed to meet. It was kind of like a date, but I encouraged a very casual meeting: at a coffee shop, jeans and sneakers required.

We hit it off and quickly became friends, and not long after we found ourselves in a budding relationship. Minus the fact that he was currently in the midst of an ugly divorce, he seemingly met all the requirements I'd set. Not only that, but he let me know right off the bat what he was looking for, what he was expecting from the person he dated, and that was what I appreciated the most. Despite our similar situations—him living at home with his parents, and me abruptly having to leave my friend's home and move in with my mother while I waited to close on my condo—we found ways to spend as much time together as possible. During this time, our relationship matured in such a beautiful way.

Yes, you read that right. My new condo. I'd finally purchased my own home, something I never thought I would be able to do, and something all of my exes assumed I would never be able to do either. I had a place to call my own. One I could put time, effort, and upgrades into without fear of walking away empty-handed like I'd done so many times before. A place that no one could take away from me or hold over my head.

I'd finally done it.

Chapter 58

My relationship with Bryan has become one of friendship. When he found out I was writing a book, he was beyond helpful on filling in the dark areas. He has paid the price for the decisions he made and is now living in a nursing home where he receives the twenty-four-hour care he needs. His relationship with Olivia is minimal but it's there, and that's more than I could hope for.

We've had some deep conversations, and he has apologized to me for the things he put me through. Being confined to a wheelchair, sitting in a room all day, he has had plenty of time to think about things, and I know his apology is genuine. Out of everyone I've dated, it's the only apology I'll receive out of the many I deserve.

Not long after we broke up, I found out that Leo had begun dating one of the local bartenders, a girl I used to work with, someone who dated a close friend of mine up until he was on his death bed. My friend told me how she left him at the hospital after he was given his cancer diagnosis, and given that he couldn't drink anymore, that was a deal breaker for her.

He filled me in on the kind of person she was, which I halfway knew already given a previous relationship she had with a married man who has since committed suicide. That guy tried to ask me out, and she got pissed and sent me a shitty message. Me being me, I don't like to get into the middle of shit, so I told the both of them to leave me out of it. After he'd committed suicide, she called around and was asking if he'd put her in his will, something his wife and family didn't appreciate. This was also something that my friend's family didn't appreciate when she called with the same question.

This was all the information that I'd told Leo back when we were still together. So, when I found out that this was the person he chose after me, I was disgusted but not surprised. They were both alcoholics; they would be perfect together. But I also knew Leo's jealousy would lead him to sit at the bar until she closed to make sure she wasn't flirting with any guys as she did nightly.

After I got news that my friend had passed away, I sent Leo a message, reminding him of what a terrible person she was. Was it necessary I do that? No. Did it make me feel better? Yes. What she did to my friend was awful. She broke his heart just weeks before he died. There is a reason she's known as the Black Widow of Valpo; it's only fair that Leo had fair warning.

I ran into them one night while I was out with some friends. I ignored them when I saw them and went about my night. My friends and I sat at a table and waited for our drinks to come. That's when I felt a tap on my shoulder. I turned around to see that it was her.

She told me that she saw everything I'd said about her, and you would think that if this wasn't true, she would have called me a liar. But she couldn't tell me I was lying because what I'd said was the truth. Instead, she told me that she would never serve me ever again.

Well, shoot, how's a girl supposed to get a drink around here? One of the other three bartenders, maybe? Fine by me!

I laughed as she walked away. Not because of what she said to me, but because I knew that Leo had brought me up in one of their arguments and used the information I'd given him as a weapon against her, just like he'd done to me so many times. I was a source of sourness between them, and it was only because I'd spoken the truth. Since then, I haven't stepped foot in that bar.

Zack ended up getting fake-married to a girl I'd met a handful of times. I say fake-married because her divorce wasn't final before they said their vows, making their marriage unofficial. They'd met during a rough period in her life, and per the usual, he saw an opportunity to take advantage of a weak woman. Convinced that he was some sort of prophet, Zack attempted to demonstrate his supposed divine powers by walking on water on Lake Michigan, only to fail miserably. After being rescued by the Coast Guard, he experienced a revelation: that this woman was an angel sent to him, and he was determined to make her his. Not long after reciting their fake vows, they had a baby, and they continued to have a volatile relationship up until late.

She finally found the courage to leave him and, in typical Zack fashion, he laid on the drama—dousing himself in gasoline in an attempt to light himself on fire. His efforts failed once again when the lighter wouldn't work. I was informed that he was putting her through the same shit he did to me and the others after me. Only this time, a sweet, innocent child was caught in the middle. Zack's mental health had only deteriorated since we briefly dated; I couldn't stand by and let him cast his spell on these people and put this child in harm's way.

I was contacted to be a character witness in her custody case against him. At first, I didn't want to get involved. It had taken me so long to get him to leave me alone. Doing this would open those gates again, and I didn't want to deal with any more harassment from him.

Yet this was my opportunity to tell my side of the story, the one that I'd kept silent while he berated me years ago. I saw this as his karma coming around to give him that swift kick in the ass he needed. When their assigned guardian called me and asked me about everything, I told him *everything.* My coming forward gave others who didn't want to do so the courage to do the same, and now this mother had a chance at getting full custody of her child and keeping them safe from a sociopath.

Sadly, I came to find out, she couldn't withstand the pressure he placed on her. They ended up getting back together and continue to live the same chaotic life. I hope it all works out for them, really, I do… strictly for the sake of their child.

I got a call from my mom one day, asking if Joel and I had gotten back together. After getting over the ridiculousness of the question, she went on to tell me how the girl he was dating looked exactly like me—so much to the point to where even my own mother thought it was me. I had to look for myself, so I looked him up on social media and they were right. She was my doppelganger.

This wasn't something only my mom and I noticed, but everyone who knew him and I did. My hair dresser, his friends I still talked to, even his ex-girlfriend before me. He definitely had a type, and his type was me.

I received news that they got married. In all seriousness, congratulations to them. I never thought he was a bad person;

he just wasn't the person for me. I hope their marriage outlives the piece of shit car that he still drives around town. Cheers to you both!

I've only run into Kyle a handful of times, typically during an annual festival our town has. Every time I do see him, he has a beer in his hand. I can only assume that he's still a functioning alcoholic and not much has changed. The girl he dated after me is usually in tow, leading me to believe that they're still in a relationship with no signs of any future commitment. I'm glad that works for them, and I'm so glad that isn't me.

Epilogue

I wake up every morning and sit on the couch sipping my coffee while scrolling through the recent arrests on my phone and reflect on how different my life could be. Even though I've been to hell and back, my belief that everything happens for a reason helped power me through. This one morning in particular, my scrolling came to a stop on a face that I'd hoped to never see again. He looked the same, only his hair had gotten grayer. He was the reason I'd constantly looked over my shoulder, wondering if he would ever fulfill the last thing he'd promised: my death.

Word was that he and the mistress had gotten divorced. I'd seen her mugshot fairly recently for domestic battery, as well. I assumed that Tom had pushed her to her limit, and she did what any girl would have done. Their divorce followed shortly after. Served them right, in my opinion. I knew karma would catch up to them one day, so I took this tidbit of info as just that.

It had been years since I'd seen his face and even still, my flight or fight response took over. He'd been arrested for grand theft auto. Again. I was sure this would be something he would weasel his way out of somehow, like he'd done so many times before. I closed the app and let my body calm down, deciding not to go on there for a few days.

I was at the gym, listening to the Dateline podcast, when a girl walked up to me, waving. I was between reps, so I took my ear pod out, looking at her, puzzled.

"Holly?"

"Yeah?"

"It's Stacy…"

I sat there, scrolling through the rolodex of names in my brain, trying to think of who she was, and then it hit me. It was her. It was the mistress.

I'd spent the past eleven years forgetting about the both of them, and here she was, right in front of me. The last time I saw her in person was when I saw red, and even then my focus wasn't on her. In the mugshot of her I'd seen not long ago, she'd been crying and had mascara running down her cheeks, so it's no wonder I didn't recognize her.

Unsure what to say, I mentioned that I heard what had happened, meaning that I'd heard they'd gotten divorced. Whether she misinterpreted my intentions or not, she immediately got defensive and accused me of taking pleasure in her misfortune. This led me to think that there was more to the story than what anyone knew. But really? Are you trying to come at me right now? I stood up from the machine I was on and met her stare head-on, ready to address the situation directly.

"Actually, I'm not that kind of person."

I still don't know what he told her about me, what lies he fed her, and what ones he was able to get her to believe. Perhaps she believed I was this terrible person he made me out to be. It was an awkward conversation, but one that ended with an apology that I hadn't expected.

"I just wanted to say I'm sorry."

I looked at her long and hard. I wanted her to say she was sorry for everything, to acknowledge the depth of her actions. Sorry for fucking my husband when she knew he was married. Sorry for lying to me when I called and confronted her. Sorry for sleeping with him in my bed while surrounded by reminders of our life together. Sorry for shattering my world, and then making me out to be the psycho.

I'd always had so much I wanted to say to her. Did she know the ring he gave her was a bad omen from the start? Originally mine, stolen from me by him, symbolizing broken vows and deceit as it once sat upon her finger? Was she aware of the agonizing truth that he sexually assaulted me and then went back home to her? Did she know that he constantly threatened and stalked me during the times she wasn't around?

"Thank you, I appreciate that."

She said goodbye and walked out the door.

I got home after the gym and did what any normal person would do: I looked that bitch up on social media and clicked on the message button. My fingers poured out everything I wanted to say—everything I thought she should know about what that man did to me and how he lied to her, too. I sent message after message until I felt satisfied with what I had said. Every hour, I checked to see if she had viewed them. A day passed, and still, no response. I opened the messages and reread them. *What was I doing?* I can only thank God for the newly implemented 'unsend' option, and I used it. I retracted all my words. Even though she never read them, it felt good to finally release what I had been holding on to for so many years.

I've gone back and forth on reaching out to her, to sit down with her and find out exactly what he'd told her about me. Whether I should make an attempt to understand the lies he'd spun around our relationship so I could make more sense of the things I went through. Regardless of what she had done to me, at least she had the balls to approach me and offer an apology apology—one I definitely thought I'd never receive.

At the same time, I'm happy now, and I don't need the closure. Part of the reason for writing my story is to let go of the things I've been carrying with me, releasing these burdens that have weighed so heavy on me for so long. The other part is to provide insight into my journey, helping people understand why I've become who I am, and why I was the way I was.

Through all the challenges I've faced, I've never seen myself as a victim, but rather as a survivor. These traumas could have easily made me bitter, soured to any potential future relationships. Instead, I've used these experiences as a tool to help me understand myself better. All of my exes have taught me one thing about myself: that I'm a kindhearted bitch with a lot of love to give. I managed to dodge bullets with these past relationships, but I also stumbled upon the one I was meant to be in. If it hadn't been for all of them turning out to be the narcissistic assholes they were, I would have never met the man of my dreams.

At the time, I didn't know that my final message on that dating app would lead me to find the love of my life. That budding connection I mentioned earlier has blossomed into a beautiful relationship. I've never known the feeling of being safe in a relationship until I met him. Gone are the days where I would find myself pleading for attention and affection. He surprises me with meaningful gifts simply because I was on his mind, not because he did something to hurt me. He's proud to be seen with me, and one of his favorite things is walking downtown hand in hand, letting everyone see us together. I can openly discuss the things I've gone through in my life with him without fear it will be weaponized against me in a future disagreement. We communicate with ease about the things that matter most to us, and I'm constantly assured of my significance and importance in his life.

Not only that, but for the first time, I'm with someone who doesn't want to be my forever boyfriend. After finding out we'd both gotten married on the same day, same year, even the same time, we joke about how we both showed up at the wrong altar. We've since promised each other to not get it wrong this next time.

As far as my relationship with my future husband is going, I haven't a single complaint. His family is great, his kids are great, and we complement each other in nearly every aspect of our lives. We have big plans to look forward to and continue to overcome any unexpected challenges that arise. It has been close to two years, and he remains consistent in everything he says and does. For once in my life, I'm not seeking an exit strategy from a failing relationship.

Our story is only just beginning.

About the Author

Residing in the northwest corner of Indiana, Holly Wells balances life as a dedicated dental hygienist and a passionate author. When she's not saving smiles or crafting stories, you'll find her exploring the great outdoors—whether it's fishing, hiking, or traveling to discover new places. Her life experiences, love for adventure and the natural world often inspire her writing, bringing a fresh perspective to her work.

The book is an important vehicle of communication which creates literary awareness in the educational society. Hope, this book will inspire all the readers especially the students and the youth. In a nutshell, Shri Ram Nivas Kumar has performed a commendable job by presenting this book.

We heartily congratulate everyone associated with this book. We wish the author all the best for his noble endeavours.

Prof. Namita Kumari
Principal, M. M. College, Patna, India

A Piece of Research Work

(Copyright reserved with the author.
Rules gladdened the University of
London.)

Knowledge of English is regarded as an index of education, and the ability to speak English correctly is regarded as an index of good schooling. Without knowledge of English, the education of a literate person may seem to be interrogated. Now learning English is an ever-growing demand. And speaking English correctly is a social requirement as well.

While we speak of spoken English, we are afraid of the correct pronunciation of the words coming to our tongue. To help readers learn pronunciation of English words, I made an intensive research; went through lots of dictionaries of international fame, found out some general rules, assembled all them and asked one to follow (illustrative not exhaustive).

First, I would like to make it clear that sound and pronunciation are not the same things. Both are somewhat different things. The sound of a particular word depends on our lung, tongue, larynx and pharynx. It also depends upon climatic condition and geographical spheres. While human mechanism is capable of producing many sounds of a single word, the pronunciation of a particular word is fixed for all and incorporated in almost all dictionaries of international fame.

There exists no single form of pronunciation which alone can be regarded as correct. The pronunciation fixed by Prof. R. K. Bansal of the University of English and Foreign

Languages, Hyderabad and Prof. A. C. Gimson of the University of London may differ from that of Collins Dictionary (Primitive/pristine). However, some general rules have been fixed for better learning:

1. Double consonants sound as a single consonant.
2. No triple vowels or consonants exist in any word.
3. Double 'cc' is pronounced either k or ks, but not otherwise.
4. B is silent before t.
5. B is silent after m.
6. L is silent before m and k.
7. S after p, k, t, f necessarily sounds s and not z.
8. S after all other consonants sounds z (Typical rule but not in practice).
9. D before j is silent.
10. G before m and n is silent.
11. There is no 'gha' sound in English.

12. There is also no 'bha' sound.

13.   H after g and b is necessarily silent.

14. Ance/ence/ant/ent sounds as ns/nt.

15. Tain is pronounced either tin or tn but not ten.

16. The ending age is pronounced iz; not ez.

17. Cious/tious at the end of a word sounds as shs.

18. Cian/sian/sion sounds as shn.

19. Cial sounds as shl.

20. D after p, k, t, f is pronounced t, not d.

21. K before n is silent.

22. N after m is silent.

23. P as word-initial with no vowel remains always silent.

24. T is silent between s and l. T is silent if comes between s and en.

25. W before r and h is silent.

26. R at the end of a word is either silent or sounded slightly (in practice but not hard & fast).

27. S after s, ss, sh, ch, g is pronounced iz, not ez.

28. D/ed after t or d is pronounced id, not ed.
29. Tion after s sounds ch. S before t is not silent.
30. G at the end of word is partially sounded.
31. G in the middle of a word is sounded in full.
32. Est at the end of a word is sounded ist.
33. C followed by s is always silent. Et after k is pronounced with the vowel I, not e.
34. In some words vowel preceding r remains silent (history, federal, founder,)
35. Pronunciation in Collins dictionary differs from that of Oxford and Chambers.
36. There is no rule for sound of a word. There is the rule for pronunciation itself.
37. If two vowels come together, works either a single one.
38. 'Th' after i is pronounced d; and after any other vowel th.

39. General rule is that two or more 'aa's, 'I's, 'o's, 'e's are not pronounced subsequently.
40. Almost all nouns may be used as verbs.
41. Every word carries some general rules of pronunciation with it.

Non-native speakers of English may not be allowed to use his or her own pronunciation. A fair amount of uniformity of pronunciation in a certain speech community is an essential social requirement. Acceptability of a certain pronunciation does not necessarily have to do with its intelligibility. Some rules are hard and fast; some are not. Some have wide-ranging acceptability. Some have been fixed for learning purposes only. There may be certain exceptions to most of the rules/points. However, to maintain a nation-wide uniformity, these rules are useful. Readers and teachers are requested to have a glance over it. Suggestions and comments are most

welcome. Clarifications, if need be, may
be sought.

-Ram Nivas Kumar
Writer of Educational Books
MA (English), MJMC, MLISc., DIP-in-OA
Malighat, Muzaffarpur, Bihar, India
Email ID-rnkddmuz@gmail.com

Speak with Correct Pronunciation

I am not here for students of English Phonetics. Hence, I am not going to teach that one. I am simply teaching rules of pronunciation, a chapter under Phonetics. I am here for educated users of English who want to speak their words correctly. I am here for students who are interested in improving their pronunciation of English words. Our motto is remediation in the matter of correctness of pronunciation.

I think you already possess a fair command of English vocabulary. But you do not know what to say on a given occasion. Your problem is not that you do not know English. The problem is also not that you cannot speak English. Your problem actually is that you have not started speaking English with correct pronunciation.

Well, you already speak in a way you can—right or even a little wrong in the matter of pronunciation of English words. You are unable to pronounce words correctly and speak English fluently. Your problem is that you speak in your own way. Your pronunciation of words is sometimes not intelligible. Hence, it is not widely acceptable. There must be uniformity in at least a certain region in the matter of pronunciation so that others can understand and get at the voice of the other persons. I am here for you to solve this problem. I will give you something that is informative and educative.

Well, there are some rules. There are some ways and manners. There are modes and methods which we should learn. Pronunciation is not a matter of regular learning. But it is certainly a matter of practice at initial stage.

And for this, I have compiled a list of words used at large, but often mispronounced. I am highly selective in choosing the materials. I have meticulously chosen the word examples that may be put to a specific rule. You should know them all. An educated person, a learner, and a good learning centre should take care of correct pronunciation.

We speak in order, by and large, to be heard and understood by others. And for this, a fair amount of uniformity of pronunciation in a given speech community is an essential social requirement, and no one can question it. Pronunciation is a matter of speaking to others and listening to them. But a speaker is not free to use his or her own pronunciation. There must be uniformity in respect of pronunciation in at least a certain speech community. Hence, learning of pronunciation is a must. That's why we are here.

The question that, we being non-native speakers of English, why should we speak like the Englishmen is not a wise question. Saying that why should we not acquire the native pronunciation of English and stick to it is not intelligible. We should be understood by the people of other states. And we should be easy to listen to them.

Knowledge of English is regarded as an index of education. And the ability to speak English correctly is an index of good schooling. This is a matter of social acceptability. It is not enough that our pronunciation is merely intelligible, but it must be acceptable to the social circle we aspire to belong to.

Usefulness of Correct Pronunciation

Correct pronunciation gives a good deal of weight in the matter of selection to certain prestigious posts. We can ill afford to ignore. This is a reality. Hence, we should use correct pronunciation. We should also keep in mind that there exists no single form of pronunciation which alone can be regarded as correct.

We are all aware of the importance of English in everyday affairs of the modern world. We are aware of the immense use of this language in the fields of trade and commerce. It is in the field of travel and tourism. English is there in administration. English is widely used in higher education. We are aware of the opportunities that knowledge of spoken English opens up. A certain amount of prestige is also attached to speaking of English.

Well, rules of pronunciation and knowledge of Phonetics are for educated users of English. Just for a simple person, this does not matter much. But I am for the students of spoken English. I am for students who already possess a fair command of English vocabulary and structure, but do not know what to say on a given occasion.

While speaking English, our pronunciation should be intelligible and acceptable. It should be there as mentioned in the advanced dictionaries of international fame. Our pronunciation should be as taught by the English scholars having expertise in this field. We may make an attempt to learn like this.

Well, based on the depth studies of advanced dictionaries of high repute, I have assembled some rules of pronunciation which fit well to English words. I have prepared a list of words commonly used but often mispronounced. We must make a practice of speaking these words correctly. These rules are not only for reference but also for regular learning.

Acceptability of a certain pronunciation does not necessarily have to do with its intelligibility. Some rules are hard and fast; some are not. Some have wide-ranging acceptability. Some have been fixed for learning purpose only. There may be certain exceptions to most of the rules/points. However, to maintain a nation-wide uniformity, these rules are useful. Readers and teachers are suggested to have a glance over it. Suggestions and comments are most welcome.

English in India is not the mother langue of a big size of population. However, prestige is attached to the learning of English. Appetite for learning English is found even among the less educated and uneducated members of the society who strive to do everything to see their children speak English so well.

English Sound and Spelling

There is not a fixed relationship between sound and spelling. The human speech mechanism is capable of producing many sounds of a single word, but all may not be true and correct. And what is correct is acceptable to all educated strata of society. Those coming through good social and educational background may put good examples of acceptable pronunciation. We should adopt them.

English alphabet has 26 letters—21 consonants and 5 vowels. English phonetics has 44 sounds—24 consonants and 20 vowels. There cannot be one to one correspondence between them. Sometimes half a dozen of letters are used for representing just one sound.

The letters "Ch" stands for different sounds: As for examples—chain, machine, monarch.

The letter "U" represents different sounds in these words—cut, put, rude, minute, bury, university.

"K" sound is represented by different letters—kit, cut, queen, account, chemistry, rock, check, fox.

Roman alphabet is inadequate for corresponding one to one sound. Hence, a letter has to represent more than one sound. To get over this problem, special phonetic script is employed in which there is a one-to-one correspondence between sounds and symbols. A given symbol represents one and only one—44 phonetic symbols—44 phonetic sounds.

Rules of Pronunciation- Rule 1 of 41

Double consonants sound as a single consonant. Examples: sunny, funny, happy, mummy/mammy, hippi/hippie, rubber, fall, arrest, affair, differ, off, bigger, hammer, bottom, assist, fuss, litter, mettle, buzz, bubble, etc.

उपर हमने सीखा कि अंग्रेजी में एक साथ आए दो व्यंजन वर्ण का उच्चारण एक व्यंजन वर्ण की तरह होता है । अंग्रेजी में संयुक्त अक्षर के उच्चारण का प्रावधान नहीं है । उदाहरण- हम sunny-सन्नी नही, बल्कि सनी कहेंगें, funny-फन्नी नहीं, बल्कि फनी बोलेंगे, happy-हैप्पी नहीं, बल्कि हैपी बोलेंगें । इसी प्रकार अंग्रेजी में बोलने वक्त हमें mummy/mammy- मम्मी को ममी बोलना चाहिए । bubble- बब्बल को बबल, और hippy/hippie-हिप्पी को हिपी बोलेंगें । silly को सिल्ली नहीं, बल्कि सिली कहेंगे । यही शुद्ध उच्चारण है ।

Reference: Oxford Advanced Learners Dictionary of Current English, 7th Edition.

Double "CC" in any word is pronounced either K or KS, but not S.

अर्थात, किसी भी शब्द में आने वाले CC का उच्चारण या तो क होता है, या कस । पर, कभी भी सिर्फ स नहीं होता ।

Examples for k: acclaim, occupant, occupy, occasion, accustom, accomplice, occur, accurate, accompany, according, etc.

Examples for ks: accede, accident, eccentric, accept, accelerate, accept, access, accessory, success, etc.

Do remember "cc" never sounds only "s" in any word. स्मरण रहे- CC का उच्चारण किसी भी शब्द में सिर्फ "स" नहीं होता ।

C is silent before e and i occurring in the middle of a word. शब्द के बीच में आने वाले अक्षर e तथा i के पहले c साइलंट होता है । Examples: descent, fascinate, fluorescent, scene, scent, science, scissors.

Rules of Pronunciation- Rule 3 of 41

There is no घ sound in English.

(Reference– A Handbook of Pronunciation of English Words, University of English and Foreign Languages, Hyderabad. Author- Prof. V. Shashi Kumar & Prof. P. V. Dhamija, Page No. 14

Hence, gha-घ should never be pronounced while speaking in English.

(Ref:- Oxford Advanced Learner's Dictionary of Current English, Seventh Edition, page- 651)

Examples: ghost- घोस्ट नहीं, गोस्ट । Ghee- घी नहीं, बल्कि गी । इसी प्रकार, ghagra-घागरा को गागरा पढ़ेंगें । ghast-घास्ट को gast-गास्ट पढ़ेंगे । ghastly को गास्टली, aghast को ऐगस्ट, ghoul को गुल पढ़ेंगे। ghat को घाट नहीं, बल्कि गाट पढ़ा जाएगा ।

Rules of Pronunciation- Rule 4 of 41

monosyllabic word- अर्थात एक पदीय शब्द (छोटे शब्द) में B before t is silent. T के पहले आने वाले b का उच्चारण साइलेंट होता है। It means if b is preceded by t, it (b) remains silent. अर्थात यदि t के पहले b हो तो b का उच्चारण नहीं किया जाता।

Examples: debt-डेट, debtor-डेटर, debut-डेव्यु, indebted-इंडेटिड (ध्यान दीजिए- यहाँ इंडेटेड नहीं, इंडेटिड होगा ।) doubt-डाउट, doubtful-डाउटफुल, doubtable-डाउटेबल, subtle-सटल, subtlity-सटलटी, etc.

disyllabic word- द्विपदीय शब्द में t के पहले b का उच्चारण साइलेंट नहीं होता है।

Examples: subtract, subtend, subterfuse, subtext, subtitle, subtotal, etc.

Make a constant practice and speak like this.

Rules of Pronunciation- Rule 5 of 41

B after m is silent. M के बाद b का उच्चारण साइलंट होता है ।

Examples: bomb-बम,   bomber-बमर, comb-कॉम, lamb-लैम, tomb-टॉम, numb-नम, thumb-थम, succumb-सकम, womb-वुम, plumb-प्लम, plumber-प्लमर, dumb-डम, limb-लिम, crumb-क्रम, climb-कलायिम, climber-कलायिमर । (शब्द समझने में सुविधा होने के लिए हिंदी में भी लिख दिए गये हैं ।) Make a practice and correct your pronunciation.

Exceptions- बहुपदीय शब्दों में यह नियम लागू नहीं होता । number, member, symbol, umbrella, crumble, fumble, humble, tumble, chamber, ambiguous, etc.

(Ref.-   Oxford   Advanced   Learner's Dictionary of Current English)

Rules of Pronunciation- Rule 6 of 41

D before g is silent.

Examples: judge, judgement, badge, bridge, budget, edge, fridge, Porridge, knowledge, etc.

D before j is also silent. Examples: adjective-ऐजेक्टिव, adjoin-ऐजोईन, adjust-ऐजस्ट, adjourn-एजर्न, adjacent-एजसंट, adjutant-एजुटन्ट, adjudicate-ऐजुडिकेट, adjure-ऐजुर, adjunct-ऐजंक्ट, etc.

Rules of Pronunciation- Rule 7 of 41

G before m and n is silent.

Examples: phlegm-फ्लेम, paradigm-पैरडीम, gnarl- नार्ल, gnash- नैश, gnat-नैट, gnaw-ना, poignant-पॉयनन्ट, compagne-काम्पेन, sign-साईन, resign-रिजाईन, malign-मलाईन, etc.

Exceptions: agnostic, signature, resignation, phlegmatic, paradigmatic, malignant.

Rules of Pronunciation- Rule 8 of 41

H at the end of a word is not pronounced.

Examples: ah! eh, oh, yeah, fatah, hurrah, Allah, etc.

"H" in all these words shall be kept silent while speaking in English.

H after r is silent.

Examples: rhea, rhyme, rhythm, rhetoric, rhotic, rhubarb, rheumatic, rhino, rhinoceros, etc.

'

Rules of Pronunciation- Rule 9 of 41

K before n is silent.

Examples: knap, knock, knack, knave, knot, knit, knee, kneel, knead, knife, knight, knob, know, knowledge, knuckle, etc.

(Don't pronounce "k" in these words. Pronounce these words starting with the letter "n" only.)

Rules of Pronunciation- Rule 10 of 41

L is silent before k and m.

Examples: walk, talk, stalk, balm, calm, palm, psalm, etc. "L" should not be tried to be pronounced. It remains always silent.

(Principle of correct pronunciation: The University of English & Foreign Languages, Hyderabad says: "What comes out so easily, effectively and effortlessly is the correct pronunciation of that particular word. Also, no single form of pronunciation is said to be the only correct. There may be two correct pronunciations of a single word which differ from region to region. Learners of English should note it down.

Rules of Pronunciation- Rule 11 of 41

N after m is silent.

Examples: autumn, column, condemn, damn, hymn, solemn. Hence, do not try to pronounce "n" in these words. N should be omitted while pronouncing these words.

Exceptions: autumnal, condemnation, damnable, solemnity, hymnal.

Rules of Pronunciation- Rule 12 of 41

P before n/s/t is silent.

Examples: pneumonia, pneumatic, receipt, psalm, psyche, psycho, psychosis, psychology, psychiatric, psychiatrist, pseudonym, Ptolemy, ptarmigan, pterodactyl, In all these words, "p" should be kept silent while pronouncing in English.

कृपया ध्यान दें- रिसिप्ट नहीं, बल्कि रिसीट।

Rules of Pronunciation- Rule 13 of 41

S before l is silent.

Examples: aisle-आईल, isle-आईल, islet-आईलट, island-आईलंड, islander-आईलंडर

Rules of Pronunciation- Rule 14 of 41

T between s and l is silent.

Examples: Castle-कासल, Thistle-थीसल, hastle-हैसल, wrestle-रेसल, wrestler-रेसलर, apostle-अपोसल, rustle-रसल, bustle-बसल, hustle-हसल, justle-जसल, whistle-विसल, bristle-ब्रिसल, mistle-मिसल, इत्यादि । Do not try to pronounce "t" occurring in such words.

इस प्रकार के शब्दों में "t" अक्षर का उच्चारण न करें । हिंदी में लिखकर अच्छी तरह समझाया नहीं जा सकता । फिर भी, आपकी अधिकतम सुविधा के लिए बतौर उदाहरण शब्द दिए गए हैं । अभ्यास कर अमल में लाने का प्रयास करें ।

Rules of Pronunciation- Rule 15 of 41

"t" between s and en remains silent.

Examples: Listen-लिसन, listener-लिसनर, listening-लिसनिंग, listenable-लिसनेबल glisten-ग्लिसन, fasten-फासन, fastner-फासनर, fastening-फासनिंग, hasten-हेसन, chasten-चेसन, Christen-क्रिसन, इत्यादि ।

Rules of Pronunciation- Rule 16 of 41

T followed by z at the end of a word is pronounced s, not z or j.

विशेष ध्यान दें – शब्द के अंत में आने वाले t के बाद z का उच्चारण स होता है, ज नहीं।

उदाहरण- glitz-ग्लिट्स, blitz-ब्लिट्स, flitz-फ्लिट्स, ritz-रिट्स, fitz-फिट्स, sitz-सीट्स, spitz-स्पिट्स, howitzer-हाउट्सर, इत्यादि।

Personal noun में भी t के बाद आने वाले z का उच्चारण "स" ही होगा, ज नहीं। Fluentzy को फ्लूएन्सी पढ़ा जाएगा, फ्लूएंजी नहीं। यही उच्चारण का नियम है। मर्म समझें, आगे बढ़ें।

There is no "Y" sound in English.

अंग्रेजी में "य" कोई साउंड नहीं होता ।

A word beginning with y, sounds J (ज). Y से शुरू होने वाले शब्द का उच्चारण "ज" से शुरू होता है ।

Examples: yes-जेस, year-जिय, yearly-जरली, yoke-जोक, young-जंग, youth-जूथ, you-जू, your-जो, yours-जोस, yourself-जोसेल्फ़, yellow-जेलो, yard-जाड, yacht-जाच, yawn-जान, yap-जैप, yeah-जीय, yearn-जर्न, yesterday-जेस्टडे, etc.

(Ref:- Oxford Advanced Learner's Dictionary of Current English, Seventh Edition, page- 1772-1777.

Rules of Pronunciation- Rule 18 of 41

There is no "Bh" sound in English.
अंग्रेजी में "भ" कोई साउंड नहीं होता ।

H after b always remains silent.
B के बाद h silent होता है ।

A word beginning with bh, sounds b.
Bh से शुरू होने वाले शब्द का उच्चारण "ब" से शुरू होता है ।

Examples: Bhagwan-बगवान, bhai-बाई, bhaji-बाज़ी, bhang-बांग, bhangra-बांगरा, bhavan-बवन, bhindi-बिंडी, Bharat-बारत, Bhubneswar-बुबनेस्व (र साइलंट है), Bharatanatyam- बरतनाट्जम (y का उच्चारण य नहीं, ज है)।

Let the pronunciation of "Bh/भ " be stopped right now.

आज से अंग्रेजी में बोलने वक्त "भ" का उच्चारण करना बंद कीजिए।

(Ref: Oxford Advanced Learner's Dictionary of Current English, Seventh Edition, Oxford University Press, Page-135.)

S after P, k, t, f/ph is always pronounced "S", and is never pronounced z/j.

P, k, t, f या ph के बाद आने वाले S का उच्चारण हमेशा ही "स" होता है, और कभी भी "ज" नहीं होता I (Taught by all distinguished and universally acknowledged dictionaries of the world. No exception.)

Examples: taps-टैप्स, stops-स्टॉप्स, maps-मैप्स, books-बुक्स, looks-लुक्स, works-वर्क्स, walks-वाक्स cats-कैट्स, rates-रैट्स, hates-हैट्स, its-इट्स, laughs-लाफ़्स, chiefs-चीफ्स, etc.

S after all other letters is pronounced j. Examples: Boys-बॉयज, girls-गर्ल्ज, airlines-एयरलाइन्ज, men's-मेंज, rings-रिंग्ज, officers-ऑफिसर्ज, etc.

If you feel difficulty pronouncing the words like native speakers, you are free to speak as per your mouth mechanism and habitual tendency. But that would be treated as having no good schooling.

Rules of Pronunciation- Rule 20 of 41

W before r is silent.

R के पहले आने वाला अक्षर- "w" साइलेंट होता है ।

Examples: wrack, wraith, wrangle, wrangler, wreathe, wrap, wrapper, wrath, wreck, wreckage, write, writer, wrest, wrestle, wrestler, wrasse, wrist, wren, wrench, wretch, wreched, etc.

W is also silent if followed by h.

W के बाद यदि h आता है, तो w साइलेंट होता है ।

Examples: who, whom, whose, whoever, whomever, whosoever, whore, whole, wholesome, etc.

Rules of Pronunciation- Rule 21 of 41

"R" occurring either in the middle or at the end of a word, if not followed by a vowel, is silent.

R, यदि किसी शब्द के बीच में या अंत में आये, और यदि उसके बाद कोई स्वर वर्ण नहीं आता है, तो साइलेंट रहता है । A typical rule. रुल टिपिकल है । सावधानीपूर्वक अभ्यास कर अमल में लाने की जरूरत ।

Examples: Art-आट,   airport-एयपोर्ट, charm-चाम,   church-चच,   park-पाक, worse-वस, herb-हब, car-का, occur-अक, hear-हीय, store-स्टो, meter-मीट, forbid-फोबिड, etc.

The letter before r has a long sound.

"र" के पहले आने वाले अक्षर का उच्चारण थोड़ी देर तक करें । Phonetic सिंबल देना सम्भव नहीं हो पा रहा है ।

R, if followed by any vowel, is not silent.

R के बाद यदि कोई स्वर वर्ण आता हो, तो साइलंट नहीं होता है ।

Examples: Radio-रेडियो, charisma-करिज्मा, carry-कैरी, occurrence-अकरेंस, hearing-हीयरिंग, storing-स्टोरिंग, aristocrat-ऐरिस्टोक्रैट, (अमेरिका में– अरिस्टोक्रैट), etc.

संदर्भ- "A Handbook of Pronunciation of English Words" by the University of English & Foreign Languages, Hyderabad, India.

s/es after s, ss, sh, g, ch and x sounds as iz. s, ss, sh, g, ch तथा x के बाद आने वाले "s" अथवा "es" का उच्चारण एस या एज नहीं होता, बल्कि ईज होता है ।

Examples: horses-हौर्सिज़, houses-हउसिज़, bushes-बुशिज़, buses-बसिज़, garages-गेरजिज़, benches-बेन्चिज़, crosses-क्रोसिज़, chooses-चुजिज़, rushes-रसिज़, messages-मेसजिज़, fetches=फेचिज़, budges-बजिज़, judges-जजिज़, churches-चर्चिज, इत्यादि ।

s/es after o is pronounced j, not s.

O के बाद आने वाले s/es का उच्चारण ज होता है, स नहीं ।

Examples: bamboos, zoos, boos, shoes, toes potatoes, tomatoes, etc.

Note: loose-लूस, (Page-909), goose-गूस, (page-670), dose-डोस, (455)

Rules of Pronunciation- Rule 23 of 41

"ed" after t or d sounds as "id".

t अथवा d के बाद यदि ed आता है तो उसका उच्चारण टेड या डेड नहीं, बल्कि टीड या डीड होता है।

Examples: Hated-हेटीड, inflated-इन्फ्लैटीड, batted-बैटीड, rated-रैटीड, wasted-वेस्टिड, elated-इलेटिड, gifted-गिफटिड, potted-पौटिड, headed-हेडीड, guarded-गाडीड (r साइलंट), raided-रैडीड, grounded-ग्रौंडीड, minded- माइंडिड, इत्यादि।

d/ed after p, k, t, f, s, ss, sh sounds as t, and not as d.

यदि p, k, t, f, s, ss, sh, के बाद d अथवा ed आता है, तो उसका उच्चारण ड नहीं, बल्कि ट होता है ।

Examples: heapedd -हिए, looked -लूक्ट, booked -बूक्ट, shocked - शॉक्ट, reached - रिच्ट, laughed -लाफ्ट, earthed -आथीट (r साइलंट), passed -पास्ट, rushed -रस्ट, meshed -मेष्ट, refreshed -रिफ्रेष्ट, oppressed - ओप्रेष्ट, depressed-डीप्रेष्ट, assessed - असेष्ट, blessed -ब्लेष्ट, dressed -ड्रेष्ट, splashed- स्प्लेष्ट, इत्यादि ।

The ending cial, sial, tial is pronounced shl.

किसी शब्द के अंत में आने वाले अक्षर समूह cial, sial, tial का उच्चारण पूर्णतः "शल" होता है; सीअल, या शीअल नहीं।

Examples: special-स्पेशल, official-ऑफिशल, initial-इनिशल, beneficial-बेनफिशल, artificial-आटिफिशल, judicial-जुडिशल, controversial-कंट्रोवशल, confidential-कॉनफिडेनशल, residential-रेजिडेनशल, prudential-प्रुडेंशल referential-रेफ्रेंशल, superficial-सुपफिशल, इत्यादि।

The word ending "cian" exactly sounds as "shn".

किसी शब्द के अंत में आने वाले अक्षर समूह "cian" का उच्चारण "शन" होता है, सियन या शियन नहीं।

Examples: electrician-ईलेक्ट्रिशन (पेज-493), politician-पॉलिटिशन (1166), magician-मजिशन (924), physician-फिजिशन (1135), academician- अकैडमिशन (7), musician-म्यूजिशन (1006), mathematician-मैथमैटिशन, optician-ऑप्टिशन, statistician-स्टेटिसटिशन, technician-टेकनिशन, beautician-ब्यूटीशन, etc.

यही उच्चारण का नियम है । ऑक्सफ़ोर्ड एडवांस्ट लर्नर्स डिक्शनरी तथा यूनिवर्सिटी ऑफ़ इंग्लिश, हैदराबाद ने ऐसा ही सिखाया है। ब्रिटेन, कनाडा, दक्षिण अफ्रीका और आस्ट्रेलिया में भी ऐसा ही होता है । जैसे ही आप "सियन" बोलते हैं, लोग समझ जाते हैं कि आपकी स्कूलिंग ठीक

नहीं है; आपकी शिक्षा समुन्नत नहीं है ।   अतः,
सही उच्चारण करने का अभ्यास करें ।

Rules of Pronunciation- Rule 27 of 41

The word ending "cious" / "tious" exactly sounds as "shs".

किसी शब्द के अंत में आने वाले अक्षर समूह "cious" / "tious" का उच्चारण "शस" होता है, सियस या शियस नहीं ।

Examples: delicious-डिलीशस (page-404), ambitious-ऐम्बिशस (45), judicious-जुडिशस (836), suspicious-सस्पिशस, superstitious-सुपस्टीशस (r साइलंट, पेज-154), malicious-मलिशस (पेज- 931) ।

लेखक का शैक्षणिक सुझाव है- इस प्रकार अभ्यास कर आपको अपना उच्चारण सही करना चाहिए ।

Rules of Pronunciation- Rule 28 of 41

The ending "age" or "dge" is pronounced "iz".

किसी शब्द के अंत में आने वाले अक्षर समूह age अथवा dge का उच्चारण "इज" होता है।

Examples: cartridge- कार्ट्रिज (पेज-227), carriage- कैरिज (225), marriage- मैरिज (941), village- विलिज-(1703), knowledge- नॉलिज (854), hostage- हॉस्टिज (753), postage- पौस्टिज (1175), porridge- पौरिज (1171), passage- पैसिज (1107), sausage- सौसिज (1348), courage- करिज (351), manage- मैनिज (932), etc.

संदर्भ- ऑक्सफ़ोर्ड एडवांस्ट लर्नर्स डिक्शनरी ऑफ़ करंट इंग्लिश (ऑक्सफ़ोर्ड यूनिवर्सिटी प्रेस)

"et" at the end of a word sounds "it", not et.

किसी शब्द के अंत में आने वाले अक्षर समूह et का उच्चारण it (इट) होता है, एट नहीं।

Examples: ticket-टिकिट, wicket-विकिट, packet-पैकिट, pocket-पॉकिट, socket-सॉकिट, locket-लॉकिट, helmet-हेलमिट, magnet-मैगनिट, racket-रैकिट, rocket-रॉकिट, basket-बासकिट, इत्यादि।

थोड़ा ध्यान देकर, और हल्का अभ्यास कर आप अपना उच्चारण अंग्रेजी के नेटिव स्पीकर की तरह कर सकते हैं।

The ending "ate" in a word (adjective or noun) is pronounced at, not et.

किसी शब्द (संज्ञा या विशेषण) के अंत में आने वाले अक्षर समूह "ate" का उच्चारण अट होता है, एट नहीं।

Examples: delicate-डेलिकट (पेज-403), temperate-टेमपरट (1580), consummate-कन्समट (328), ultimate-अल्टीमट (1657), fortunate-फॉचुनट (r साइलंट, पेज- 612), deliberate-डिलिवरट (403), delegate-डेलिकट, intricate-इंट्रीकट, predicate-प्रेडिकट, syndicate-सिंडीकट, etc.

संदर्भ- ऑक्सफ़ोर्ड एडवांस्ट लर्नर्स डिक्शनरी ऑव करंट इंग्लिश (ऑक्सफ़ोर्ड यूनिवर्सिटी प्रेस)

Rules of Pronunciation- Rule 31 of 41

The ending "tain" in some words sounds as either tin or tn.

किसी शब्द के अंत में आने वाले अक्षर समूह tain का उच्चारण कुछ शब्दों में टिन होता है; कुछ में टन।

Examples: captain-कप्टीन (पेज-220), mountain-माउंटन (997), fountain-(फाउंटन-613), curtain-कटन (r साइलंट, पेज-376), certain-सटन (r साइलंट-239)

In verbal words, it shall be pronounced "ten" क्रियाजन्य शब्दों में इसका उच्चारण टेन होगा। इसे समझदारी पूर्वक ग्रहण करें:

Sustain-सस्टेन (ट पर जोर), maintain-मेन्टेन, pertain-पटेन, entertain-इन्टटेन (r साइलंट होगा)।

Such is the correct pronunciation of these words. just make practice and speak like this.

यही इन शब्दों का स्तरीय उच्चारण है । इसे अभ्यास कर अमल में लाएं।

Rules of Pronunciation- Rule 32 of 41

S before "tion" is not silent. It sounds definitely. अक्षर समूह "tion" के पहले आने वाले s का उच्चारण साइलंट नहीं होता । इसका उच्चारण निश्चित रूप से किया जाता है ।

Examples: suggestion-सजेस चन- 1535), question-केस चन (1235), digestion-डाइजेस चन- 425), congestion-कनजेस चन (320), etc.

इसी प्रकार Christian- क्रिस चन (261) होगा । यही इन शब्दों का सही उच्चारण है । बात देखने में छोटी लग सकती है, पर जानकारी बड़े महत्व की है । अंग्रेजी के उच्चस्तरीय छात्र भी इसका उच्चारण करने में भूल कर रहे हैं । आप इसी प्रकार शुद्ध बोलने का अभ्यास करें। अंग्रेजी पढ़ें, आगे बढ़ें ।

The ending "en" is pronounced exactly like "an".

किसी शब्द के अंत में आने वाले अक्षर समूह "en" का उच्चारण एन नहीं, बल्कि "अन" की तरह होता है। अर्थात, हम listen को लिसेन नहीं पढ़ेंगे, बल्कि इसे लिसन पढ़ा जाएगा।

Examples: listen-लिसन (897), glisten-ग्लिसन (658), hasten-हेसन (612), fasten-फासन (557), spoken-स्पोकन (1478), chasten-चेसन (249), moisten- मइसन (985), इत्यादि।

अंग्रेजी का उच्चारण k से क, kh ख के सिद्धांत पर आधारित नहीं है। किसी consonant के बाद o आने से इसका उच्चारण निश्चित रूप से "ओ" नहीं होता। इसी प्रकार e आने से "ए", और i के आने से "ई" नहीं हो जाता। इसका उच्चारण एक विशिष्ट तरीके से निर्धारित है। समझदारी पूर्वक ज्ञान ग्रहण करें।

The ending "ence" in long words (having two or more syllables) does not pronounce ence. Rather, it is pronounced "ance".

किसी शब्द के अंत में आने वाले अक्षर समूह ence का उच्चारण एंस नहीं, बल्कि अंस होता हैं । आप भी ऐसा ही बोलकर अपना उच्चारण शुद्ध करें । उदाहरणस्वरूप कुछ शब्द नीचे दिए गए हैं-

Reference-रेफ्रंस (1269), difference-डिफ्रंस (डे नहीं डि, 423) deference-डेफ्रंस (डि नहीं डे,401) preference-प्रेफ्रंस (1186), essence-इसंस (518), beneficence-बिनेफिसंस (130), relevance-रेलवंस (1278), prominence-प्रोमिनन्स (1208), perseverance-पसिवरन्स (r साइलंट, 1126), confluence-कनफ्लुअंस, audience-अडिअंस(86), ambience-ऐम्बिअंस (45), affluence-ऐफलूअंस (26), absence-ऐबसंस (पेज- 04), इत्यादि ।

The ending "ent" is pronounced ant, and not really ent.

किसी शब्द के अंत में आने वाले अक्षर समूह ent का उच्चारण एंट नहीं, बल्कि अंट होता हैं। यह अंग्रेजी उच्चारण का नियम है । इसे यूनिवर्सिटी ऑफ़ लन्दन की स्वीकृति प्राप्त है । ऑक्सफ़ोर्ड डिक्शनरी में यही बताया गया है । यूनिवर्सिटी ऑफ़ इंग्लिश, हैदराबाद ने भी यही सिखाया है । आप भी इसी प्रकार अभ्यास कर शुद्ध उच्चारण प्रारंभ करें ।

Examples: different-डिफरंट/डिफ्रंट(423), resistent-रेजिसटंट   (1292),   inclement-इन्क्लेमंट (785), impotent-इम्पटंट (780), virulent-विरलंट (1705), insolent-इन्सलंट (804),   insolvent-इन्सोलवंट   (804) indolent-इन्डलंट (791), insurgent-इन्सजंट (r साइलंट 807), imminent-इमिनंट (776), etc. (Reference- OALD)

The adjectival word ending "est" does not sound est. Rather, it sounds ist.

विशेषण शब्द के अंत में आने वाले अक्षर समुह "est" का उच्चारण एस्ट नही, बल्कि इस्ट होता है |

Examples: hardest-हार्डिस्ट, farthest-फादिस्ट, darkest-डार्किस्ट, longest-लॉगिस्ट, largest-लार्जिस्ट shortest-शॉटिस्ट, softest-सॉफ्टिस्ट, hottest-हॉटिस्ट, coolest-कुलिस्ट, brightest-ब्राईटिस्ट, harshest-हार्शिस्ट, blackest-ब्लैकिस्ट, tempest-टेम्पिस्ट (1580), harvest-हार्विस्ट (711).

आप भी इसी प्रकार शुद्ध उच्चारण करने का अभ्यास करें । यकीन माने, यदि आपने उपरोक्त बताई गई सभी बातों को ग्रहण कर लिया तो बहुत बड़े विद्वान भी आपको बोलने वक्त एक बार देखेंगे जरुर । इसलिए, अंग्रेजी पढ़ें, आगे बढ़ें |

If you want to be a cut above the rest,
Learn English, Move Forward.

Rules of Pronunciation- Rule 37 of 41

The last letter of a word sounds slightly. It means the last letter in a word is a weak sound. It is always unstressed. It may or may not be heard clearly.

किसी शब्द के अंत में आने वाले अक्षर का उच्चारण हल्का होता है। अर्थात, किसी शब्द का अंतिम अक्षर उच्चारण की दृष्टि से कमजोर होता हैं। इस अक्षर पर ज्यादा जोर नहीं दिया जाता। इस अक्षर का उच्चारण यदि सुनाई न भी दे, तब भी इसका उच्चारण सही माना जाएगा। यह आपके ज्ञान पर निर्भर करता है कि आप इस शब्द को सुनने के बाद सही ढंग से समझ पाते हैं, या नहीं।

Examples: ring-रिंग, sing-सिंग wing-विंग, sling-स्लिंग, sting-स्टिंग, etc.

last-लास्ट, vast-वास्ट, past-पास्ट, cast-कास्ट, mast-मास्ट, etc.

and-एंड, band-बैंड, land-लेंड, sand-सैंड,

kind-काइंड, find-फाइंड, bind-बाइंड, mind-माइंड, etc.

इन सभी शब्दों में अंतिम अक्षर g, t व d का उच्चारण हल्का होगा । हो सकता है- आपको सुनाई न भी दे । पर, इसका उच्चारण शुद्ध और सही माना जाएगा । यही अंग्रेजी उच्चारण का नियम है । आप भी इसी प्रकार ज्ञान ग्रहण कर आगे बढ़ें ।

Learning English is a must. Hindi won't do; English will.

C is silent before e and i.

यदि e और i के पहले c आए, तो यह साइलंट रहता है।

Examples: scene,   scent,   descent, fluorescent, science, scissors, fascinate, etc.

C is silent in the above words. Hence, don't try to pronounce c.

उपरोक्त सभी शब्दों में c का उच्चारण साइलंट है। अतएव, c का उच्चारण करने का प्रयास न करें।

C is pronounced like s if followed by e, i or y.

यदि c के बाद e, i या y आता है, तो c का उच्चारण s (स) की तरह होता है।

Examples: century, cement, ceremony, cent, centre, central, cite, circle, cycle, cyclone, etc.

Rules of Pronunciation- Rule 39 of 41

Generally, e at the end of a word has the least role in pronunciation of that particular word. E at the end has no sound.

सामान्यतया, किसी शब्द के अंत में आने वाले स्वर वर्ण (Vowel) "E" का उच्चारण में कोई रोल नहीं होता है । अतएव, E का उच्चारण करने का प्रयास न करें ।

Examples: caste, taste, etiquette, core, more, lore, pore, shore, rate, etc.

(Exception- extempore-एक्स्टेम्परी, page-539, Larvae is pronounced larvi (लावी).

Generally "g" followed by a, o, & u is pronounced ग.

यदि g के बाद a, o, u आता है, तो g का उच्चारण ग होता है।

Examples: gang, gold, gun, etc.

If g is followed by e, i, & y (not hard and fast), it is pronounced ज।

यदि g के बाद e, i, y आता है, तो इसका उच्चारण ज होता है।

Examples: Gel, ginger, energy, surgery, etc.

Exception- get-गेट

g at the end always sounds ग.

शब्द के अंत में आने वाले g का उच्चारण हमेशा ही ग होता है।

Examples: bag, bug, dig, etc.

If g is followed by consonants r and l, it is pronounced g.

यदि g के बाद consonants r या l आता है, तो इसका उच्चारण भी ग होता है।
Examples: great, grapes, glass, glow, etc.
यद्यपि कि ग और ज के उच्चारण में हमें ज्यादा दिक्कत नहीं होती, तथापि हमें इस प्रकार सीखना चाहिए।
We often mispronounce "corrigendum". The letter g sounds j, not g.

"corrigendum" का आमतौर पर लोग गलत उच्चारण करते हैं। इसे कॉरिगेंडम नहीं, बल्कि कॉरिजेंडम पढ़ा जाना चाहिए।
(Reference– Oxford Advanced Learner's Dictionary, 7th Edition, Page No.- 343)

Rules of Pronunciation- Rule 41 of 41

In a nutshell, we can say that:

The pronunciation of a word depends on/upon one's larynx. It depends on pharynx. It depends on one's lungs. It depends on one's tongue. It also depends on one's mouth mechanism.

Pronunciation depends on sound production technique one evolves. It depends on one's speaking habit one develops. It depends on tongue twisting style one adopts. It also depends on climatic condition and geographic sphere one lives in.

While speaking in English and pronouncing different words, one must remember that no single form of pronunciation can be said to be the only correct. There may be two or more than two correct pronunciations of a single word.

Variation in sound of a word does not mean it's a wrong pronunciation. We know—no two persons can make sound all alike. Differences in pronunciation of certain words by the people residing in different regions are natural phenomena.

The principle is that what comes out so easily, effectively and effortlessly is the correct pronunciation of that particular word. It is globally acceptable.

Tips to Pronounce a Word Correctly

We can learn the same things again in different ways:

Rule #1: Short words have short vowels

Vowel sounds are commonly divided into short and long vowel sounds. While they may seem complicated, there are some rules for knowing when a vowel sound is short or long.

Short vowels always occur in short words. These are often one syllable and typically have three or four letters as in "cat", "tin" and "bend".

Rule #2: Two vowels side-by-side make a long vowel

Two vowels beside each other are not uncommon in English, but they can be easily mastered with this simple trick.

Namely, when there are two different vowels beside each other, they generally make the long sound of the first vowel. For example, the word "meat" has the long *e* sound, the word "plain" has the long *a* sound and the word "goat" has the long *o* sound.

Rule #3: Keep vowels short before double consonants

Double consonants don't only have rules for how they are pronounced, but also play a role in how to pronounce the vowel that comes before them.

The rule is simple: the vowel that comes before double consonants is always in its short pronunciation. To see this, let's look at the difference in pronunciation between the words "diner" and "dinner."

The word "diner" has only one *n*, and the *i* is pronounced as a long vowel. Conversely, the word "dinner" has double *n*, so the *i* is pronounced as a short vowel.

Rule #4: Pronounce double consonants as a single letter

Unlike some languages, double letters in English are not pronounced any different than single letters.

This is true for words that have double *ll*, *ss*, *ff*, *rr*, *pp*, *zz*, *dd* and *cc*. They are all pronounced as if they are singular such as the words "fuzz," "occur," or "fluff."

Rule #5: Pronounce double consonant *TT* as *D*

In General American English, there is one double consonant that is not pronounced like its singular counterpart. In fact, the double consonant *tt* gets reduced to what sounds like a *d* sound.

This can be seen in the pronunciation of the words "little" and "letter."

Rule #6: If *E* is at the end of a word, it's silent

Sometimes English words can be confusing if they end an *e*. Many learners will want to include the *e* in their pronunciation, but it is actually silent.

Rather, the *e* causes the vowel before it to become long such as "ate," "bite," or "rope."

Rule #7: Pronounce *C* like *S* when it's followed by *I, E,* or *Y*

C makes more of an *S* sound when it is followed by *i, e,* or *y* such as words like "cite," "century" and "cycle."

Rule #8: Pronounce the word ending *TION* with a *SH* sound

The word ending *tion* is tricky to pronounce for two reasons.

The first reason is that the *t* is not pronounced like a *t* at all. Instead, it is pronounced like a *sh* as in the word "shoe." Next, the vowels in the ending are reduced to a schwa. As a whole, *tion* ends up being pronounced more like "shun."

This gives us words like "tradition", "situation" and "position" that include the *sh* sound followed by a reduced schwa vowel.

Rule #9: *G* and *K* are always silent before *N* at the beginning of a word

Many languages have rules that every consonant must be pronounced, but English has many rules that make consonants silent in certain cases.

One of these rules is that when a word begins with a *k* or a *g* and then is immediately followed by an *n*, the *k* or *g* is not pronounced. Instead, it's almost as if the word started with a *n*. This can be seen in words such as "knee," "knock" and "gnarl."

Rule #10: Pronounce *S* like *Z* at the end of a word

There are many situations where the letter *s* is pronounced like a *z* sound.

This happens when a word that ends in a *b, d, g, l, m, n, ng, r, th* or *v* becomes plural or an *s* is added.

Examples of this include the plural words "moms" or "kings" and the *s* in words like "there's" and "Michael's."

The *es* ending of plural words is also pronounced like a *z* as in the word "buses."

Rule #11: Pronounce *S* like *Z* between two vowels

When *s* is between two vowel sounds, it is pronounced like a *z*. This gives us words like "phase," "music" and "please."

There are some exceptions to this rule, such as in the words "goose" and "chase."

Rule #12: Pronounce *X* like *GZ* before a stressed syllable

By now, we know that *x* makes a *ks* sound as in "taxi" or "toxic." But this sound is only in unstressed syllables.

When *x* comes before a stressed syllable, it can make a *gz* sound as in "examine" or "exist."

Rule #13: Pronounce *X* like *Z* at the beginning of a word

There is yet another way that *x* can be pronounced.

Rarely, it can make a *z* sound as in the words "xylophone" or "xenophobia." This pronunciation happens almost exclusively at the beginning of words (unless you're saying the word "x-ray").

Rule #14: *Y* is both a consonant and a vowel

Y is a unique letter in English. It acts like both a consonant and a vowel.

When *y* is at the beginning of a word or syllable, it is considered a consonant. In these cases it is pronounced with the long *ee* sound like in the words "young," "you" or "beyond."

When *y* is at the end of a word or syllable, it is a vowel and can be pronounced a few different ways.

Y sounds like a long *e* sound at the end of a word such as in adverbs like "quickly" or "slowly." This pronunciation happens mostly in adverbs (words ending in *ly* that describe verbs) or words that end in *ity* like "community" or "ability".

Y sounds like *ai* in one syllable words such as "fly" or "cry."

It sounds like a short *i* sound in words where it is in the middle of a syllable like "gym" or "cyst."

When combined with *a*, the *ay* combination is pronounced like a long *a* sound as in "play" and "day."

Rule #15: *NG* sometimes sounds like two letters stuck together

When learning English, we learn that the *ng* combination makes a special sound as in the words "king" or "thing."

There is, however, a second pronunciation of *ng*. In fact, there are certain words where the *ng* is not pronounced as a singular sound, but rather pronounced in such a way that you hear both letters: *n* and *g*. Some of these words are "anger," "finger" and "hunger."

Rule #16: Unstressed vowels make a "schwa" sound

While a "schwa" may seem like a fancy English sound, it's actually not. In fact, it is the sound that is easiest for our mouths to create; holding the jaw slightly open, relaxing the tongue and making a short sound. It is very similar to the short *u* sound in English.

The cool thing about the "schwa" is that it can happen to virtually any vowel. When a vowel is unstressed in a word, it reduces to this sound. This can be seen in the words "pand**a**," "mitt**e**n," "b**i**kini," "citr**u**s" and "freed**o**m."

Rule #17: Past tense endings aren't always pronounced as *D*

The regular past tense in English is formed by adding *ed* to the end of verbs. This ending, however, can be pronounced multiple ways.

The first way is as a general *d* sound. This happens for verbs that end in voiced consonants (consonants that use the vocal cords) like *n, m, g, l, z, b, r* and *v,* and this results in the words "rolled," "rubbed" and "revved."

The second pronunciation of the *ed* ending is as a *t.* This happens for verbs that end in voiceless consonants (consonants that don't use the vocal cords) like *k, f, s* and *p.* This results in the words "kicked," "flopped" and "huffed."

The third pronunciation of this ending is pronounced like *id* with a short *i* sound.

This pronunciation is for verbs that already end in a *t* or a *d* as in "fitted" or "skidded."

Rule #18: Sometimes *H* is silent

Most of the time, when an *h* is at the beginning of a word, we pronounce it by almost letting out a little sigh, such as in "hot" or "humble."

There are a few words in which you don't let this little bit of air out and rather pronounce the word as if there is no *h* at all such as "honor" or "hour."

Rule #19: Pronounce *OO* as a short *U* when it's followed by *K*

Usually, the *oo* combination is pronounced with a long *u* sound such as in "school" or "doom," but sometimes it has a short *u* sound. This occurs when it is followed by a *k* such as in "look" or "book."

Rule #20: Pronounce *Ei* as a long *E* if it comes after *C* in a stressed syllable

Usually *ei* is pronounced as the long *a* sound such as in "neighbor" or "weight." The exception to this is when *ei* follows a *c* in a stressed syllable such as words like "receive" or "fancies."

Rule #21: Pronounce *S*, *Z* and *G* like a French speaker in specific words

Believe it or not, the French language had a big impact on the way English words are written and pronounced. One of the most evident French sounds in English is in some words with *s*, *z*, or *g*.

Z is pronounced this way in words such as "seizure." *G* can also make a French *j* sound as in the word "regime" or as in the second *g* in the word "garage."

S can have a French-like pronunciation in words like "vision" and "measure." This sound is pronounced like the French *j* as in the French word je (I).

This sound is pretty rare and only occurs in specific words. I recommend memorizing these words as there is no rule for when the sound should be made.

Rule #22: *OU* has many pronunciations

You would expect *ou* to be pronounced almost like "ow" in most cases such as with words like "about," or "shout." There are also quite a few instances when this does not apply and the *ou* combination is pronounced differently.

If the combination is *oup*, a long *o* sound is formed, such as "soup" or "group."

With *ould*, a schwa sound is created and it sounds more like *ood* with not much of an *l* sound like in "would" or "could."

If the combination is *ough*, there is a variety of pronunciations, depending on the word. It can sound like there's an *f* at the end such as in "cough" or "rough." It could also just sound like a long *o* such as "through." Lastly, if the combination is *ought*, it can sound like "ot" such as the world "thought."

These ones can be a bit difficult and memorization is the best way to remember which words make which sounds with the *ou* combination.

Rule #23: Stress on the first syllable makes the word a noun

Word stress doesn't only affect the pronunciation of some letters, but it also changes the meaning of some words. As a matter of fact, changing the stress on some words changes them from nouns to verbs.

When word stress is on the first syllable of some words, that word is in its noun form. When stress is on the last syllable, that word is in its verb form.

This can be seen in the words "**pro**duce" (noun form) and "pro**duce**" (verb form) as in "the farm pro**duces** a lot of **pro**duce" and the words "**in**crease" (noun form) and "in**crease**" (verb form) "we have to in**crease** our sales to see an **in**crease in profit."

Rule #24: *L* becomes dark near the end of a syllable

The letter *l* has two pronunciations referred to as the "clear *l*" and the "dark *l*."

"Clear *l*" is the common pronunciation of the letter that we are used to as in the words "leave," "loose" and "pluck." The "dark *l*" is pronounced by raising the back of the tongue during pronunciation.

This often occurs when *l* is at the end of a syllable as in the words "pull" and "milk." This rule also applies to words that end in *le* as in "little" and "nibble." In these words, it almost sounds like there is a "schwa" preceding the "dark l" sound.

Rule #25: *TH* can be voiced or unvoiced

Even though *th* is taught as a sound that is somewhat unique to English, its complication doesn't stop there. In fact, the "th" in English is pronounced as two distinct sounds.

The first "th" sound is voiced (vocal cords vibrate) as in the words "though," "then" and "they."

The second "th" is voiceless (vocal cords do not vibrate) as in the words "thought," "thick" or "cloth."

Unfortunately, there is no rule for when to use which sound. That means that you will have to memorize which words have which sound.

Don't fear weird English pronunciation! By learning these simple rules, you can master English speaking and communicate clearly to whoever you meet!

Learners are suggested to make a good practice of the words keeping in view the rules concerned.